THE BATTLE OF THE *Java Sea*

SEA BATTLES IN CLOSE-UP · 16

THE BATTLE OF THE *Java Sea*

F. C. van OOSTEN

LONDON
IAN ALLAN LTD

First published 1976

ISBN 0 7110 0615 6

Published by Ian Allan Ltd, Shepperton, Surrey.
and printed in the United Kingdom by
Biddles Ltd, Guildford, Surrey

Contents

Preface

The Battle of the Java Sea, viewed strategically, had little impact on the course of the war and yet it has left its scars on history. If ever a battle was fought against hopeless odds it was those naval engagements fought at the end of February and at the beginning of March 1942. I speak deliberately of engagements for we must consider not only the battle between the Combined Striking Force and the Japanese Fleet on February 27th, 1942, but also the Battle of Bantam Bay and the fatal last battle between the *Exeter* and her two destroyers, and the four Japanese cruisers with their escort. These last two battles were the direct result of the fight on February 27th, 1942. The Japanese themselves refer to the battle on the 27th as the sea battle near Surabaya, first phase; the battle of Bantam Bay as the sea battle near Batavia and the engagement with the *Exeter* as the sea battle near Surabaya, second phase.

The account of the Battle of the Java Sea and the period before and after this naval action has been compiled mainly from official Dutch reports and papers, but Japanese, American and British papers have also been studied.

In the Bibliography only a few of the books used as a secondary source have been mentioned. The photos come mainly from the Naval Historical Section of the Naval Staff at the Hague, though some have been supplied by the Rijksinstituut voor Oorlogsdocumentatie at Amsterdam.

I would like to thank the artist Mr J. P. M. Wanders for the maps and diagrams which he kindly drew to clarify some parts of the text; Messrs T. M. Boere and H. Jonker for their search in the various photographic archives to discover some photos which had not been published before—a task which was carried out in good humour, without the use of too many unprintable naval expressions, and Mr A. M. Rog for carrying out a lot of spadework in the dust of the naval archives whereby some hidden data can now be brought to the surface. I must also show my appreciation to my wife for reading through the text and saving me from drowning in the treacherous eddies of English grammar! But first and foremost I am grateful to Captain A. G. Vromans RNLN (retd) who laid the cornerstone, without which this book could not have been written, and who reconstructed the track of the ships during the battle on February 27th. This chart differs entirely from the track charts published up until now, but shows surprisingly little differences from the Japanese reconstruction! Unless otherwise stated all times are Java-time (GMT plus 7½ hours). The Japanese used Tokyo-time (GMT plus 9 hours). For geographical names the English spelling has been used; where a name was spelled with *oe* in Dutch, this has been substituted by *u* in English. This practice has not been followed in the spelling of names of persons and ships. For the spelling of the names of Japanese ships the Hepburn system or classic system has been used.

F. C. van Oosten,
Voorburg,
Holland.

PART I
THE BATTLE

Introduction

"We had to defend ourselves against a very powerful enemy and the aid of our allies was still problematical." *(Admiral C. E. L. Helfrich in his Memoires, Volume 1)*

Though on May 10th, 1940 the Netherlands entered the war in Europe and became an ally of Great Britain, it was not until the end of that year that the two countries began to discuss military and maritime problems in the Far East in the event of hostilities in the Pacific area. On October 31st, 1940 the Netherlands government agreed to an informatory exchange of ideas, but the British on the other hand did not want to be bound by mutual agreements. For this reason agreement was not reached until December 5th, 1941.

From November 25th to 29th, 1940 staff-talks were held in Singapore between British, Australian and Dutch officers, while American officers were present as observers. The talks were held under the direction of Vice-Admiral Sir Geoffrey Layton, Commander-in-Chief China. In the United States in the meantime Admiral H. R. Stark, Chief of Naval Operations, had on November 12th, 1940 advised President Roosevelt to allow representatives of the navy and army to start secret talks with the British, which could lead to plans and agreements. Stark stressed the point, however, that in case of war the Atlantic area should be the most important theatre of operations for the United States. After Roosevelt had approved this idea an invitation was sent to London for talks in Washington.

The conference commenced on January 29th, 1941. On the American side there were present Admiral H. R. Stark, Rear-Admiral R. L. Ghormley, Rear-Admiral R. K. Turner and General G. C. Marshall; on the British side there were the chiefs of staff and Rear-Admiral R. M. Bellairs, and also representatives from New Zealand, Canada and Australia.

This conference, to which the Netherlands were not invited, was concluded on March 27th with the so-called ABC-1 Staff Agreement. Under discussion came the problems in the Pacific, and Great Britain and the United States reached an agreement over the strategic principles which would apply in the Far East should war break out with Japan. The Atlantic Ocean and Europe would be considered the main theatres of war, while in the Far East a defensive strategy would be followed. In other words the American forces in that area would not be considerably strengthened. The Pacific Fleet on the other hand would be allowed to pursue an offensive strategy. The slogan for this policy was 'Help beat Hitler first'.

The Washington talks were to form the basis for the continuation of this conference which was to take place in April 1941 in Singapore. Meanwhile Great Britain, Australia and the Netherlands had been together in Singapore from February 22nd to 25th. During this so-called ADA-conference (Anglo-Dutch-Australian), which was held under the chairmanship of Air Chief Marshal Sir Robert Brooke-Popham, Commander-in-Chief Far East since November 18th, 1940, American officers were present as observers. The conference concluded that a large scale attack on Australia and New Zealand could not be carried out as long as Singapore was available as a base.

In London there was a feeling that it would be justifiable to issue a statement to the effect that the United States, Great Britain and the Netherlands had concluded an alliance. It was believed that such a statement might restrain Japan from committing an act of aggression. However, this did not appeal to the United States, especially as they were still carrying out negotiations with Japan. On the other hand they believed in continuing the military talks to work out strategic plans in the Pacific and in the Far East.

These talks were held from April 21st to 27th, 1941 in Singapore. While this ADB-conference (American-Dutch-British) was being held, a BD-conference (British-Dutch) was also taking place. During these conferences strategic plans were worked out for the protection of the possessions in the Far East of the participating countries against a

Japanese attack. The main topics of the discussions were the safeguarding of the sea lanes and the defence of Singapore as the most important bastion.

On August 1st, 1941 the British Minister for Foreign Affairs, Anthony Eden, told the Netherlands ambassador in London that the British would give complete support to the Netherlands in case of Japanese aggression. Later that month there were talks between the chiefs of staff of the United States and Great Britain during the Atlantic Conference held between Churchill and Roosevelt on board the *Prince of Wales* in Argentia. The results of the ADB-conference were revised and changes were introduced which resulted in an ADB-2-agreement. On the whole there were but few changes. However, the ADB-2, dated August 30th, 1941, was not approved by Washington.

It was now decided that, in view of the dispatch of British capital ships to Singapore, the British and Americans would discuss ADB-2 in Manila in December 1941. The Dutch would also be invited at a later date. But the course of events prevented the conference from taking place.

Meanwhile Queen Wilhelmina had instructed her Minister for Foreign Affairs to inform Tokyo that if Japan extended her southward aggression the Netherlands would not look on passively. Nothing, however, was said of the possibility of war if Japan did move south.

On November 12th, 1941 the Commander-in-Chief China issued the Plans for the Employment of Naval and Air Forces (including Army Air Forces) of the Associated Powers in the Eastern Theatre in the Event of War with Japan (shortened to Plenaps), which were based on the Singapore conversations of April 1941. The aim of the Plenaps was to inform the countries concerned in the Far East about the agreed strategic plans for the use of naval and air power. This could also lead to the working out of operational plans for this area. Operational orders based on these plans would be further issued by local commanders. There were four Plenaps: Plenap A when there was no indication as to which territory Japan intended to attack; Plenap B when an attack on Malaya appeared to be imminent or was developing; Plenap C when an attack on the Philippines was developing or appeared to be imminent;

Plenap D when an attack on Eastern Borneo, or the Netherlands East Indies, by way of the Eastern Archipelago, appeared to be imminent or was developing.

As a consequence of the British-Dutch talks of April 1941 one cruiser, two destroyers and two submarines of the Netherlands Navy would come under the command of the Commander-in-Chief China, as it was assumed that the United States would remain neutral. The cruiser would be employed as an ocean escort for convoys on the Singapore-Fremantle route; the destroyers could be used as an anti-submarine escort for convoys and for patrols in Sunda Strait, while the submarines were to operate in the South China Sea, south of the line Cape Padaran-Kudat, and carry out offensive actions. On November 30th, 1941 the Netherlands government in London decided that two submarines should report to the Commander-in-Chief China the next day. The British government issued a statement on December 5th, 1941 that she was prepared to co-operate to the full with all available means to repulse any attack in the Far East. The following day the Commander-in-Chief China received a message from London that Great Britain would receive American aid should the British and the Dutch be attacked by the Japanese.

At 01.55hrs on December 8th, 1941 Pearl Harbour was bombed; nearly an hour earlier Japanese troops had landed in Malaya. At 05.00hrs Davao was bombed, while half an hour later the Japanese landed in the Philippines. At about 08.00hrs the Netherlands government declared war on Japan, one and a half hours later followed the Japanese declaration of war on the United States and Great Britain. At 19.00hrs London declared war on Japan followed by Washington at 09.30hrs on December 9th. It was not until January 11th, 1942 that Japan declared war on the Netherlands!

Since December 8th, 1941 the Japanese had advanced very rapidly and booked many victories. On Christmas Day Hong Kong had fallen, while on January 2nd, 1942 Manila and Cavite were occupied. The way lay open to push further south.

CHAPTER ONE

The Japanese Advance Towards Java

The Situation on January 10th, 1942

"the retirement or weakening of Britain in that area might well lead to the disappearance of Holland from the map of the Far East and the end for the existence as a colonial power." *(P. T. Etherton and H. Hessell Tiltman in* Japan, Mistress of the Pacific?)

When dawn broke on January 10th, 1942 the situation in the Netherlands East Indies—"that girdle of emeralds" as the nineteenth century Dutch author Eduard Douwes Dekker (1820-1887) had called it—looked pretty grim. The Japanese were much interested in the Netherlands East Indies, because here they would find the raw materials, especially oil, which they needed to continue the war. The Japanese advance to the south had moved more quickly than anticipated at Imperial Headquarters at Tokyo and as soon as British North Borneo, Davao and Jolo had fallen into Japanese hands, it could be expected that they would move towards the Dutch island empire.

The general idea was that three forces would attack the East Indies: a Western Force, concentrated in Camranh Bay and intended for the attack on South Sumatra, Banka and Palembang and, after the fall of the latter place, Western Java; a Central Force, concentrated at Davao, for the capture of Tarakan, Balikpapan, Bandjermasin and finally Eastern Java; an Eastern Force, also concentrated at Davao, for the capture of Menado, Kendari, Ambon, Makassar, Timor and Bali. The Japanese invasion army destined for the Netherlands East Indies was the 16th Army under the command of Lieutenant-General Imamura.

Various naval landing forces were attached to the army (for details see Appendix 1).

The army would be transported and escorted by the navy, known as the Southern Force, under the command of Vice-Admiral Nobutake Kondo, Commander-in-Chief of the 2nd Japanese Fleet (for details see Appendix 2). Air support was supplied by the 3rd Air Division of the Army Air Force, which had to support the Western Force and the 21st and 23rd Air Flotillas of the 11th Air Fleet of the Naval Air Force under the command of Vice-Admiral N. Tsukahara, as well as the 1st Air Fleet of the Naval Air Force under the command of Vice-Admiral Nagumo (for details see Appendix 3).

A Combined Command is Set Up

"In order to ensure immediate co-ordination and co-operation in our common effort against the enemy, there is being established a supreme commander for all British, Dutch and American forces in the South-West Pacific theatre." *(President Roosevelt in a telegram to Marshall Chiang Kai-shek)*

January 10th saw the first attempt to create a combined command in the Pacific. On this day General Sir Archibald Wavell arrived in Java and the same afternoon a conference was held at Batavia. The general situation in the South-West Pacific was reviewed and the initial organisation of the ABDA-command (American-British-Dutch-Australian) was set up. The idea for this command had been born during the first Washington conference held from December 23rd, 1941 to January 14th, 1942 between Roosevelt and Churchill. During this so-called Arcadia-conference the possibility of the "unity of command in the Far East" was discussed, with the result that General Sir Archibald Wavell was appointed Supreme Commander. The directives were issued on January 3rd, 1942 and on the 4th he received these in New Delhi. This united command came, however, too late, for by the time that it started to function, both Tarakan and the north-east part of Celebes were occupied by the Japanese.

The strategic aim of the ABDA-forces was to hold the

Malay Barrier in the line of Malaya-Sumatra-Java-Lesser Sunda Islands-Australia. At noon on January 15th the ABDA-command began to function at Batavia. The Supreme Commander, General Wavell, had as his deputy Lieutenant-General G. H. Brett (US Army Corps) and as his Chief of Staff Major-General Sir Henry R. Pownall. Commander of the Naval Forces (ABDA-float) was Admiral T. C. Hart USN with Rear-Admiral A. F. E. Palliser as his deputy and Chief of Staff. Commander of the Ground Forces (ABDA-arm) was Lieutenant-General H. ter Poorten with Major-General Sir Ian S. Playfair as his deputy and Chief of Staff; Commander of the Air Forces (ABDA-air) was Major-General L. H. Brereton (US Army Air Corps), who was relieved on January 28th by Air-Marshal Sir Richard E. C. Peirse, with Group-Captain L. Darvall RAF as his deputy and Chief of Staff.

From a Netherlands point of view it was disappointing that only one Dutch officer was taken up in this command. The East Indies were certainly the richest and strategically most important territory in the ABDA-area and undoubtedly the sea-area was best known to the Dutch, yet not one of their officers had a top appointment in the Naval Forces Command. Admiral Helfrich was particularly disappointed and in his memoirs he says that he "felt bad". As Commander-in-Chief of the Royal Netherlands Navy in the Netherlands East Indies he had to stay at his headquarters in Batavia and there was no direct contact with Lembang. He was never asked for any advice and the only way in which he was kept informed of the allied plans was by the Dutch naval officer on the staff of ABDA-float.

An important but most unfortunate change was that the shore-based Netherlands Naval Air Service was placed under the command of the Air Force in concurrence with the British organisation where all shore-based aircraft came under the Royal Air Force, while aircraft on board carriers and other warships came under naval command. In this case the transfer meant that the navy had lost its "eyes" and that all the prewar training between ships and aircraft had been in vain.

On January 18th the headquarters of ABDA-command

were moved to the Grand Hotel at Lembang near Bandung which was safer from air or sea attack. Fourteen days later ABDA-air moved from Lembang to Bandung when it became clear that the former place lacked sufficient accommodation. On January 24th, at the request of General Wavell, the ABDA-area was slightly enlarged by including Port Darwin, the service base of the United States Navy, and the north-west coast of Australia, "as was necessary for a successful defence against enemy landings, and for air operations from a base in that area" (see Map 1).

All in all it can be stated that the command organisation was too complex. ABDA-air was in Bandung (since February 1st, 1942), ABDA-float was in Lembang, communications were inadequate and to top it all the staff of the Royal Netherlands Naval Air Service was in a different building from that of ABDA-air. A sound co-operation between the navy and the air force was thus impossible. A single war room had never been established and the commanders of the three ABDA-forces were therefore unable to take quick decisions. The administrative control over the forces remained with the national commanders, so that the ABDA-command was a purely operational command. The allied national commanders were: United States: Admiral T. C. Hart (navy), Major-General J. F. Barnes (army), General L. H. Brereton (air); United Kingdom: Commodore J. Collins RAN (navy), Lieutenant-General A. E. Percival (army), Air-Marshal Sir Richard E. C. Peirse (air); Netherlands: Vice-Admiral C. E. L. Helfrich (navy), Lieutenant-General H. ter Poorten (army) and Lieutenant-General L. H. van Oyen (air).

Changes in the Japanese Plans of Operation

"Well, war has begun at last. But in spite of all the clamour that is going on we could lose it. I can only do my best." *(Admiral Yamamoto in a letter to his sister)*

Before coming to the actual advance of the Japanese forces into the East Indian archipelago it must be noted that at the end of December 1941 Imperial Headquarters had made

Top: The motor torpedo boat 5 launches a torpedo. This boat took part in the Battle of Badung Strait. On March 8th, 1942 she was destroyed by her own personnel.

Above: Troops of the Royal Netherlands East Indies Army with a Japanese flag, which was captured near Palembang. The photo was taken at Batavia.

Top left: After a Japanese attack on Andir airport, near Bandung, on February 17th, 1942 some allied aircraft are left as smoking remnants.

Bottom left: A blockship obstructs the entrance to Perak Harbour at Surabaya.

Top: Demolition work is carried out in Oosthaven (Sumatra).

Above: The Japanese light cruiser *Naka*, which, with the *Jintsu*, belonged to the Sendai class. They were launched in 1924 and 1925, but were modernised in 1934 and 1941. The *Naka* was sunk on February 17th, 1944 about 35 miles west of Truk by aircraft from the American carriers *Bunker Hill* and *Cowpens*.

Above: The American destroyer *Stewart* capsized in dry-dock in Surabaya, where she had to undergo some repairs after the Battle of Badung Strait. During a bombardment of the naval port on February 24th, 1942 the ship received one hit. On March 2nd, 1942 she was demolished, but the Japanese repaired her and commissioned her as Patrol-boat 102. After the war she returned to the USN and sank as a target off San Francisco on May 24th, 1946.

Below: The Australian cruiser *Perth*.

Above: During the bombardment of Surabaya on February 24th, 1942 the merchant vessel *Kota Radja* was hit by Japanese bombs and caught fire. On the right the surveying vessel *Willebrord Snellius*, which was sunk as a blockship on March 6th, 1942 in the entrance to the naval port of Surabaya.

Below: Bombardment of Surabaya by the Japanese. The naval establishment is seen on the left of the canalised River Mas, on the right is the Royal Netherlands Naval Air Station Perak.

Above: A capsized aircraft-dock in the port of Surabaya.

Top right: After a Japanese bombardment on Surabaya some sheds on the naval establishment are on fire.

Middle right: A view in the roads of Surabaya a few days after the bombardment by Japanese aircraft on February 24th, 1942. The merchant vessel *Kota Radja* is still burning. A Netherlands destroyer is making its way to the naval establishment. On the right the bows of the *Houston* can be seen.

Bottom right: The last conference of Admiral Doorman with his commanding officers and staff officers at Surabaya on February 26th, 1942. The conference was held at the Aniem-building (office of the electrical company). Doorman stands at the end of the table and gives operational details for the coming events. Near the door stand Cdr. J. A. de Gelder, chief of staff, and Lt A. F. Baron van Tuyl van Serooskerken, aide-de-camp. Both officers were killed in the Battle of the Java Sea. The watercolour was painted by J. H. Hoowij for Commander A. Kroese RNLN (retd).

Above: The flagship of Rear-Admiral K. W. F. M. Doorman, the *De Ruyter.*

Below: The Netherlands cruiser *De Ruyter* ready to depart for sea. In the foreground Dutch troops.

Top right: The Japanese heavy cruiser *Haguro,* sistership of the *Myoko, Ashigara* and *Nachi* (Myoko class). The ships were designed by Vice-Admiral Y. Hirago. Before war broke out the ships, launched in 1928 and 1929, were twice modernised, in 1936 and in 1939/1941. During the second period the torpedo-armament was increased from 12 to 16 tubes, while the new 60.9cm Long Lance torpedo was installed. The *Ashigara* took part in the naval review at Spithead in 1936 on the occasion of the coronation of King George VI. The *Haguro* was sunk on May 16th, 1945 by five British destroyers, 55 miles west-south-west of Penang.

Middle right: A Catalina aircraft flying over the roads of Surabaya, which can be seen faintly in the background.

Bottom right: Action stations aboard the *Tromp.* The 40mm anti-aircraft is manned and ready to fire at attacking aircraft.

Top: The *Perth* is firing a salvo. The original painting by J. W. Heyting was presented by the Royal Netherlands Navy to the Royal Australian Navy on June 9th, 1948 at Melbourne.

Above: The British destroyer *Jupiter* (G 85) shown with her sistership *Kashmir* (ex-*Javelin,* G 12). Both ships were lost at sea, the *Kashmir* on May 23rd, 1941 during the Battle of Crete, the *Jupiter* on February 27th, 1942 during the Battle of the Java Sea.

Right: A drawing by J. H. Hoowij, showing the moment that the four remaining cruisers of the Combined Striking Force passed the survivors of the *Kortenaer.* The British destroyer *Encounter* was detailed to pick them up and then to return to Surabaya. The ships sail in line ahead, *De Ruyter* leading, followed by *Perth, Houston* and *Java.*

Top: The burning harbour installations of Perak in Surabaya after a Japanese bombardment.

Above: The Netherlands destroyer *Evertsen* beached on the island of Sebuku Besar in Sunda Strait.

Top: The end of the *Exeter* after her gallant fight against a strong Japanese force.

Above: Damage to the naval establishment at Surabaya after a Japanese bombardment.

Top: At the beginning of March 1942 naval personnel started to demolish their own naval base at Surabaya. Ships which were unable to leave were scuttled.

Above: The Netherlands destroyer *Banckert* was damaged by a near-miss on February 24th, 1942 and had to enter a floating-dock for repairs. Four days later she was hit again by a bomb. On March 2nd the submarine *K XVIII* fired a torpedo on the dock to demolish the ship and the destroyer. The result was that the dock capsized. The *Banckert* was repaired by the Japanese and commissioned as Patrol-boat 106. After the war she was found again, but as she could not be repaired she was used as a target for gunnery purposes. In September 1949 she was sunk in Madura Strait during gunnery exercises.

Top right: The surrender talks at Kalidjati on March 8th, 1942. On the left Lt-Gen H. ter Poorten.

Bottom right: Japanese troops enter Surabaya on March 8th, 1942.

Above: The minelayer *Abraham Crynssen* managed to escape from Surabaya on March 6th, 1942. She had an adventurous journey and escaped the Japanese by being camouflaged as an island. In this photograph the ship is waiting for nightfall in a bay of Sumbawa Island. On March 15th, 1942 she arrived in Geraldton.

Below: The Netherlands cruiser *Tromp* after her repairs in Sydney. The light cruiser was damaged during the Battle of Badung Strait in which ten men were killed and 30 badly wounded. After provisional repairs in Surabaya the ship was directed to Australia. Next to the *Ark Royal* the *Tromp* was a ship 'which was sunk the most'. Japanese radio broadcast that she was sunk five times and therefore the Australians nicknamed her the 'ghostship'.

some alterations to its plans of operation. Some of these alterations were:

(1) The date for the capture of Ambon was brought forward (from February 6th to the end of January);
(2) Portuguese Timor, occupied by the allies on December 17th, 1941, had to be taken by Japanese forces;
(3) The occupation of Bandjermasin should take place over land and not by sea due to a shortage of warships to escort the transport ships to Bandjermasin.

During the second half of January it was decided that the airport on Bali had to be occupied, as aircraft based at Celebes and Borneo were continually up against bad weather and the airport at Den Passar was excellently situated to harass and destroy the allied air forces.

The Japanese Begin Their Advance

On January 10th, 1942 two Japanese landing forces were under way from Davao, where the Central Force had left on January 7th, destination Tarakan, and the Eastern Force on January 9th for the attack on Menado.

Tarakan had been bombed regularly by Japanese bombers since December 24th, 1941 and on January 10th, 1942 Dutch aircraft based at Tarakan sighted the Japanese invasion fleet consisting of 16 transports and the necessary escort. In the early hours of January 11th the Japanese landed at three points to occupy the airport and the oilfields. As related before, it was on this day that Japan declared war on the Netherlands in order to protect Japanese citizens and interests in the Netherlands East Indies!

After a day and a half of hard fighting the Japanese had reached their objectives and caused heavy casualties amongst the defenders. At about 07.30hrs on January 12th the Commanding Officer Tarakan decided to surrender. This message of surrender, however, did not reach the coastal battery Karungan, as the telephone lines had been cut and after the surrender this battery sunk two Japanese minesweepers, the *W 13* and *W 14,* which, with four other minesweepers, were sweeping the southern approaches to the harbour. For this "offence" the Japanese killed the entire crew of the battery! Work on the destruction of the oil installations, harbour works and airfield had begun on January 10th and 100,000 tons of stored oil were set on fire which filled the night with an eerie light and heavy black smoke.

The Dutch minelayer *Prins van Oranje,* which had laid a minefield in the southern approaches, the submarine *K X* and one patrol boat made use of the darkness to make their escape during the night of the 10th and the early morning of January 11th. The minelayer, however, was discovered and sunk by the Japanese destroyer *Yamakaze* and patrol boat 38.

The Eastern Force had reached the north-eastern part of Celebes—also called Minahassa—between midnight and dawn on January 10th the troops landed at five points: two near Menado; near Tanah Wangko; in the Amurang Bay and near Kema. The next day Menado fell while the Japanese landed special naval airborne troops (334 men) south of Lake Tondano, near the airfield Langoan, and again a day later 185 men were dropped at the same place. In the meantime Dutch, American and Australian aircraft had attacked the invasion fleet off Kema with the loss of one Dutch Catalina and negligible results.

On January 13th all key positions were in Japanese hands. Menado proved to be of great importance to them, because on January 24th Headquarters of the 21st Air Flotilla were moved to the Minahassa. After the capture of Tarakan and Menado the Japanese prepared their next step. The Central Force had to advance on Balikpapan and the Eastern Force towards Kendari. Balikpapan, like Tarakan, was important for its oil, while to the north there were coalmines.

On January 21st the Japanese troops left Tarakan. On its way south this force was attacked on January 23rd by Glenn Martin bombers of the Army Air Force which sank the steamer *Nana Maru* (6,764brt). That same evening the ships anchored near Balikpapan. Before midnight the submarine

K XVIII managed to torpedo one of the anchored troop transports, the *Tsuruga Maru* (6,988brt).

Later during the night four American fourstackers, *John D. Ford, Pope, Parrott* and *Paul Jones,* approached the anchorage at high speed to attack the invasion fleet. They were guided by the burning oil installations of Balikpapan, which, together with the airfield, had already been destroyed and blown up on January 20th and 21st and which gave the additional advantage that the Japanese ships were clearly silhouetted against the flaming sky.

Between 03.00 and 04.00hrs they sank three transports—the *Sumanoura Maru* (3,519brt), *Tatsukami Maru* (7,064brt) and *Kuretake Maru* (5,175brt), and damaged one patrol craft, the *P 37.* For the United States Navy this was the first action by surface ships since 1898. Despite these Allied successes the Japanese advance was not delayed for even one day.

Between 03.00 and 06.30hrs on January 24th the Japanese landed their troops at two points and soon the Commanding Officer Balikpapan received permission from General Headquarters at Bandung to withdraw his garrison. After a difficult journey these men—about 200 in number—arrived at Samarinda airfield, where they were used for the defence of this field. Samarinda airfield, about 120 miles west of the town of Samarinda, was not known to the Japanese until January 24th when a transport aircraft was shot down by three Japanese fighters shortly after takeoff. The next day it was bombed by a large Japanese force. The oilfields near Samarinda were destroyed on January 20th after news had been received that the Japanese were getting ready to move south from Tarakan. Eleven days later the Dutch troops left Samarinda for Tenggarong. On February 3rd the Japanese occupied Samarinda. Slowly the Dutch troops withdrew to the airfield, closely followed by the sons of Dai Nippon.

On March 6th there was a short clash with about 400 Japanese troops near Muaramuntai. Two days later it was all over.

Simultaneous Moves of the Eastern and Central Force

"Victories will be exploited to break the enemy's will to fight." *(From Operational Order Number 1 issued by Admiral Yamamoto on November 5th, 1941)*

The Eastern Force kept in step with the Central Force when the assigned Japanese troops embarked in six troopships on January 21st from the island of Bangka, north of Celebes. The same day this force set course for Kendari. The Japanese became interested in this town when in the course of 1940 an airfield, the best one in the Netherlands East Indies, was constructed about six miles west of it.

The invasion force anchored near Kendari on January 24th at about 03.00hrs and at sunrise the troops landed. The resistance put up by the defenders was weak and the same day the airfield fell into Japanese hands, a heavy blow for the Allies as they would soon learn. From Kendari East Java was now within reach of the Japanese bombers.

After Kendari, Ambon was the next target on the Japanese list and as already mentioned the date of attack had been brought forward from February 6th to the end of January. Ambon was defended by troops of the Netherlands East Indies Army and by Australian troops, while Dutch, Australian and American planes were based at Halong (seaplanes) and Laha. Before the actual invasion Ambon had been bombed several times. On January 16th four groups of eight bombers and four fighters appeared over the island and damaged the seaplane base beyond repair.

The Dutch and American Catalinas were withdrawn to Surabaya. The day Japanese troops landed at Kendari, aircraft from the carriers *Soryu* and *Hiryu* (17 bombers and 18 fighters, their first mission after their participation in the attack on Pearl Harbour) attacked Ambon. On January 25th nine Japanese bombers destroyed hangars and petrol installations at Laha airfield. The next day four fighters destroyed three Australian Hudsons, while one was damaged. On January 28th all serviceable aircraft were withdrawn.

The troops for the conquest of Ambon were embarked at Davao on January 27th and they sailed for the island via

Menado. Three days later the transport ships anchored near Hitulama on the north coast and Rutung on the south coast. Early in the morning of January 31st the troops landed. With negligible resistance the town of Ambon was captured the same day, while the next day Australian troops defending a coastal battery surrendered. Laha airfield was captured on February 2nd and with the exception of two infantry sections in the northern part of the island, the rest was in Japanese hands by February 3rd. The infantry sections waged a guerrilla warfare for four days, but were then forced to surrender. The navy scored a small indirect success. Minefields in the Bay of Ambon, which were laid by the *Gouden Leeuw,* a sistership of the *Prins van Oranje,* were responsible for the loss of a Japanese minesweeper, the *W 9,* while two minesweepers, the *W 11* and *W 12,* were damaged. On February 5th the Japanese began to base aircraft at Ambon and again the area in which the Japanese had air supremacy had been extended. Thus while the Eastern Force had moved closer to the Malay Barrier, the Central Force had also made one step forward. After the capture of Balikpapan the need arose to capture the airfield of Ulin, about 16 miles south-east of Banjermasin, which was more convenient for the air actions against Java. As their invasion fleet had suffered heavy losses at Balikpapan the Japanese were sure that even bigger losses would be suffered at Bandjermasin, still closer to the Dutch airfields on Java. Also, the Barito River was too shallow for their transports and the navy had insufficient escort ships.

The Japanese therefore decided on the following plan of operations: the transports which took part at the landing at Balikpapan would bring the troops for Bandjermasin to Tanahgrogot. The ships would then sail for Palau to refuel. The main force of the troops would march on to Bandjermasin overland, while an amphibian force would move down the coast in landing craft—sailing only at night to ensure secrecy—to land at a point about 50 miles SSE of Bandjermasin.

On January 30th the troops which were to attack by land left Balikpapan and the next day they landed at Tanahgrogot. The amphibian forces had already left

Balikpapan on January 27th. The land-forces marched for nine days through dense jungle and during this march 80 per cent of the Japanese troops suffered from malaria. On February 10th the airfield at Ulin was captured, while the same day Bandjermasin also fell into Japanese hands. In both these cases the land-forces worked in close co-operation with the amphibian forces, which had landed without opposition on February 8th.

The last place to be captured by the Japanese outside the Malay Barrier was the port of Makassar. The Japanese forces embarked on February 6th at Kendari. At midnight on February 8th/9th the transports anchored south of Makassar while the troops landed on the 9th. The same day Makassar was occupied. Resistance was negligible, but the Dutch troops withdrew into the interior where they started a guerrilla warfare.

This invasion force had been reconnoitred on February 8th by the American submarine *S 37*, which had managed to make an attack on the ships, sinking the Japanese destroyer *Natsushio*. At 19.00hrs the Naval Officer in Charge Makassar had given orders to destroy the harbour installations. The demolitions were completed 2½ hours later. On February 9th the Japanese were preparing for their assault on the Malay Barrier.

Allied Activities in the Archipelago

"It was a race against time and the enemy was too quick for us." *(General Sir Archibald Wavell)*

Before relating the final approach of their forces which led to the capitulation of the Netherlands Indies on March 8th it is necessary to review events in the other parts of the archipelago.

One of the main duties of the ships of the allied navies operating in the Indian waters was the escorting of convoys and single merchantmen. Especially important in these days were the convoys to Singapore, where the situation was getting worse.

Ships and aircraft carried out anti-submarine patrols and

reconnaissance flights. Japanese bases and ships were being bombed whenever possible. Aircraft were used for evacuating military personnel from places where no more damage could be inflicted on the Japanese to positions where they could again take part in the defence, and for rescuing men from shot down aircraft and from ships sunk by the Japanese. Allied submarines were working hard in the search for the aggressor.

On February 2nd an important decision was taken at Lembang to form a Striking Force the next day. Talks for the formation of this force had already started in the second half of January in order to facilitate attacks on Japanese ships in the Makassar Strait. General Wavell and his Chief of Staff were greatly in favour of the idea, but Admiral Hart and Admiral Palliser were against it. In the end, however, they agreed.

The Striking Force would consist of the following ships: *Houston, Marblehead* and the 58th Destroyer Division (Stewart, Bulmer, Barker, Edwards), *De Ruyter, Tromp, Van Ghent, Piet Hein* and *Banckert*. The force, which, in the coming weeks, varied in composition, came under the command of Rear-Admiral K. W. F. M. Doorman on board *De Ruyter*. On February 3rd Surabaya was bombed for the first time by Japanese bombers from Kendari. Other places were also attacked by aircraft causing serious losses. In total the navy lost 12 aircraft, the army 18. Even worse was the fact that these aircraft had sighted the ships of Admiral Doorman in the Madura Strait. On February 4th the Striking Force set course for the Makassar Strait but they were bombed near Kangean by three groups of nine Japanese bombers flying at about 12,000 feet. Both American cruisers were hit and had to set course for Tjilatjap to carry out repairs. *De Ruyter* sustained slight damage. The planned operation to Makassar Strait was cancelled. Makassar town could be taken.

Four days later the Striking Force assembled at Tjilatjap where a conference was held with Admiral Hart on board *Houston*. The same day the Dutch ships of the force left harbour and set course for Makassar Strait when it became

Map 1
Limits of ABDA-command
USSR
MANCHURIA
KOREA
135°
CHINA
Shanghai
RYUKYU IS.
FORMOSA
Calcutta
BURMA
Canton
Hong Kong
INDIA
HAINAN
LUZON
Rangoon
INDO-CHINA
SIAM
Manilla
Bangkok
NICOBAR IS.
Saigon
Cam-ranh Bay
PHILIPPINE IS.
CEYLON
Colom-bo
ANDAMAN IS.
Davao
MALAYA
Brunei
Tarakan
Singa-pore
Kuching
BORNEO
Batavia
Indian Ocean
JAVA
Surabaya
TIMOR
Kupang
COCOS IS.
Darwin
90°
105°
AUSTRA

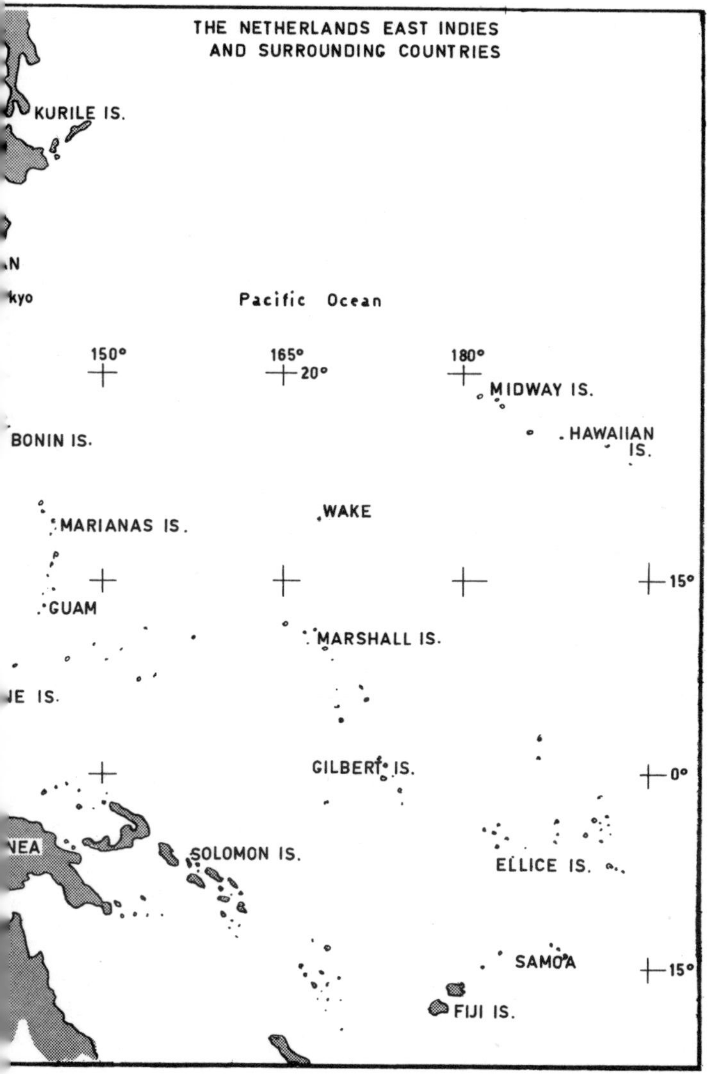
THE NETHERLANDS EAST INDIES
AND SURROUNDING COUNTRIES
KURILE IS.
N
kyo
Pacific Ocean
150°
165°
20°
180°
MIDWAY IS.
BONIN IS.
HAWAIIAN IS.
WAKE
MARIANAS IS.
15°
GUAM
MARSHALL IS.
IE IS.
GILBERT IS.
0°
NEA
SOLOMON IS.
ELLICE IS.
SAMOA
15°
FIJI IS.

known that a Japanese naval force had been sighted at the south-east point of Celebes.

Thus was the situation a week before the surrender of Singapore on February 15th.

The Western Force Strikes at South Sumatra

"From the air aspect defence of Java is a hard matter; without Southern Sumatra it is formidable." *(General Wavell in a letter to Churchill)*

In the meantime the Japanese Western Force was preparing itself for the advance into the western archipelago. Since the fall of Balikpapan there was only one oilfield left, Palembang on the east coast of Sumatra. Everything had been done to step up oil production and to withhold the area from the Japanese by all possible means.

On January 27th the first Japanese troops of the Western Force landed on Dutch territory at Pamangkat (Borneo) and two days later Pontianak and the airfield Singkawang II were taken. For air operations against Banka and Palembang the Japanese intended to use the airfields at Kuantan (Malaya) and Kuching (British Borneo). Due to the fact that the former airport could not be readied in time, the date of attack on Banka and Palembang was moved from February 10th to the 15th. Originally the Japanese High Command had been of the opinion that these attacks could only be started after Singapore had been captured. However, if Palembang fell into Japanese hands it meant that Singapore would be entirely cut off.

The Japanese forces earmarked for the attack on Banka and Palembang consisted of an Advance Force and a Main Force under Vice-Admiral Ozawa. The Advance Force was intended for the occupation of strategical points on Banka, such as the airfield near Muntok. After this it would be split up into three forces which were to attack Palembang via tributary streams of the Musi River which led to this important harbour. The Main Force was detailed for the attack on Palembang and South Sumatra. Due to their swift approach in the Malayan peninsula the Japanese had attained air supremacy in this part of the archipelago. During the first half of February the bombardments on airfield Palembang I—about 10 miles north-west of Palembang—increased in intensity. The airfield Palembang II—about 40 miles south-west of Palembang—had not yet been discovered by the Japanese. Much shipping in the waters between Singapore and the Java Sea was attacked and sunk by Japanese aircraft.

February 9th saw the departure of the Advance Force from Camranh Bay, two days later followed by the Main Force. On February 14th the Malay Barrier was attacked for the first time by Japanese troops, when at approximately 08.30hrs about 700 paratroopers from the 1st Parachute Brigade, under command of Colonel Kume, who came from an airfield at Sungaipatani (Malay), were dropped at three places near Palembang. The Japanese had learned their lesson at Tarakan and Balikpapan: they wanted the oilfields undamaged and they succeeded in so far as the demolition of some oil refineries near Pladju was not carried out according to plan.

The same day the Advance Force landed on Banka and took Muntok airfield without opposition. Part of these forces sailed up the mouth of the Musi River at daybreak.

The Striking Force Sets out to Intercept the Japanese Invasion Fleet

"All Admiral Helfrich wanted to do was put to sea and hunt Japs." *(Major-General L. H. Brereton USA)*

Meanwhile both invasion fleets had been sighted by submarines and aircraft. The reconnaissance signals made ABDA-float decide to concentrate the Striking Force. On February 13th the ships of this force made a rendezvous at Oosthaven. The next day at 16.00hrs the force—*De Ruyter, Hobart, Exeter, Tromp, Java, Van Ghent, Kortenaer, Piet Hein, Banckert, Stewart, Barker, Bulmer, Edwards, Pillsbury* and *Parrott*—steamed north. The general plan was to attack the Japanese force, which had penetrated the South China Sea, when they were reported off the east coast of Banka or the west coast of Billiton.

The Striking Force would sail through Gaspar Strait

along the north coast of Banka and then through Banka Strait back to Tandjong Priok. In the early hours of February 15th a Dutch destroyer—the *Van Ghent*—ran aground on a reef and had to be destroyed by its own crew. At 09.20hrs the Striking Force was spotted by an aircraft from the *Chokai;* 2½ hours later the first air attack took place in which the cruisers were the main target.

Admiral Helfrich, in his new function of ABDA-float, asked for air protection, but not one allied fighter appeared in the skies above the Striking Force, while 22 Hurricanes of the Royal Air Force were available at Palembang II airfield This may have been caused by a lack of co-ordination in the ABDA-command, but it could also be due to the Japanese attack on Palembang which made it impossible to provide the allied fleet with air protection. As it was Admiral Doorman decided to turn back at 13.20hrs. The force was attacked a total of five times during the day, but when the last aircraft had disappeared at about 17.45hrs the allies had suffered no losses from the Japanese.

Meanwhile the Main Force, which was on a southerly course when the Striking Force was sighted, had changed course to the north. Admiral Ozawa decided to attack the allies with all available aircraft. However, after Admiral Doorman had turned about, the Main Force changed course again to the south and in the evening of February 16th the invasion fleet steamed up the Musi River at high tide where that same evening Palembang had been taken by troops of the Advance Force.

The situation in the East Indies was now rapidly deteriorating. On February 15th, Black Sunday, Singapore capitulated. By the end of the next day the Japanese were in possession of the precious oilfields near Palembang. Relentlessly they pressed on towards Benkulen and Telukbetung, which were taken on February 25th.

A Change in Command

"I did the best I could with what I had, and under the conditions present. I was defeated. That's all there was to it." *(Admiral Thomas C. Hart USN)*

On February 11th, in the meantime, there had come as a

complete surprise for the non-initiated the information that Admiral T. C. Hart, at his own request, wanted to lay down his command "because of ill health". Vice-Admiral C. E. L. Helfrich was to succeed him and in accordance with this decision of the Combined Chiefs of Staff in Washington the official transfer of command took place on February 14th.

After the fall of Singapore General Wavell had to report to the Combined Chiefs of Staff that the Malay Barrier could not be held without substantial reinforcements. However, this was impossible, as priority had been given to the European theatre of war. The loss of Singapore and the Philippines had split the vast ABDA-area into two sections, which were widely separated: Burma and the north-west coast of Australia.

Then on February 21st General Wavell received a message from the Combined Chiefs of Staff to the effect that Java "should be defended to the last by all combatant troops then on the island". Reinforcements for the naval and air forces which were underway were allowed to go on to their destination, but the army reinforcements had to be re-directed. Also the ABDA-headquarters on Java had to be withdrawn.

A day later General Wavell discussed the decision with the governor-general and at last it was decided that the following proposal would be sent to Washington: ABDA-headquarters would not be withdrawn, but dissolved and the command over the naval, army and air forces in the Netherlands East Indies would be handed over to the Dutch. The Combined Chiefs of Staff agreed to this plan and on February 25th, at noon, ABDA-command ceased to exist and a new organisation came into force. The allied naval force now came under the operational command of Vice-Admiral C. E. L. Helfrich together with the Striking Force (Rear-Admiral K. W. F. M. Doorman RNLN), the rest of the Asiatic Fleet (Vice-Admiral W. A. Glassford USN) and the rest of the China Force (Commodore J. A. Collins RAN). The name Asiatic Fleet had actually been changed on January 30th, 1942 to United States Naval Forces in the South-West Pacific. The army came under the command of Lieutenant-General H. ter Poorten, while the allied air forces, now organised in the so-called Java Air-Command, had already (on February 22nd), been put under the command of Major-General L. H. van Oyen. The air force was placed under the overall command of General Ter Poorten. All three commanders were stationed in Bandung. But time was too short to carry out the reorganisation, which was so necessary for an efficient direction of the war. This meant that Admiral Helfrich was still unable to command aircraft for reconnaissance purposes at sea. On March 1st, 1942 the total disintegration of the allied naval command followed with the departure of the American and British commanders, while a day later Admiral Helfrich departed for Colombo. The defence of the remnants of the Netherlands Indies against the Japanese force seemed an immense, almost hopeless and ungrateful task. Nevertheless it was decided, maily on internal political grounds, to carry on to the bitter end.

The Position of the Governor-General of the Netherlands East Indies

"Without shame we can look back upon the past year." *(The Governor-General of the Netherlands East Indies on May 10th, 1941)*

According to Article 62 of the written constitution of 1938 the King was charged with the supreme direction of the Netherlands East Indies, while the Governor-General carried out the instructions given to him via the minister for the Colonies. In Article 6 it is stated that the navy is an instrument of the state. In the constitution for the Netherlands East Indies it was laid down that the Governor-General was the Supreme Commander of the Royal Netherlands Navy and the Royal Netherlands East Indies Army.

What influence did the institution of ABDA-command have on the position of the governor-general as commander-in-chief? For the Supreme Commander, General Wavell, would, in the new situation, be superior to the governor-general. The Netherlands government in London, had therefore asked A. W. L. Tjarda van Starkenborgh Stachouwer how he imagined his position would be with regard to the Supreme Commander. It was decided not to pursue this matter at all.

On January 15th, 1942 the governor-general stepped down as operational supreme commander and, only temporarily, took administrative control over the Netherlands and the Netherlands East Indies forces. This situation remained until February 25th, 1942 when the ABDA-command was dissolved and Wavell handed back the supreme command in the Netherlands East Indies to the governor-general. The supreme command, however, did not include the allied forces, as these were put under the command of the Commander-in-Chief Naval Forces in the Netherlands Indies and the Commander-in-Chief of the Royal Netherlands East Indies Army in their capacity as allied supreme commander of the respective forces. Because of possible difficulties, which, at the capitulation, could result from the fact that the governor-general was also supreme commander of the Netherlands forces, this functionary handed over at 13.00hrs on March 4th, 1942 the supreme command in the Netherlands Indies to Lieutenant-General H. Ter Poorten and Rear-Admiral J. J. A. van Staveren. The latter had temporarily taken over the duties of the Commander-in-Chief Netherlands Naval Forces in the Netherlands Indies after Admiral Helfrich had left Java on March 1st, 1942. What was left of the American and British naval forces in the Indies after March 4th was placed under the command of General Ter Poorten.

The Japanese Attack the Eastern Part of the Malay Barrier.

"It was [now] clear that Japan was a most formidable and dangerous antagonist." *(Memorandum of the British Cabinet)*

Before the final attack on Java the Japanese had planned to capture two more places in the eastern part of the Malay Barrier: Timor and Bali.

It has already been mentioned that Dutch and Australian troops had occupied Portuguese Timor on December 17th, 1941. The decision for this action had been taken, because the Japanese had shown an unhealthy interest in this part of the island since the beginning of 1940. By this means the allies intended to prevent the Japanese from obtaining a stronghold in their rear. Furthermore Timor was an important link in the air route between Australia and Malaya and the connections between Australia and the Netherlands Indies generally.

The Portuguese government was informed by the allies that they had no territorial ambitions whatsoever and that they would withdraw their troops as soon as the Portuguese had taken the necessary measure for the defence of Dilly. The Portuguese troops, sent out in February, never reached the island; the Japanese beat them to it.

From February 12th the Japanese stepped up the air bombardments of the airfield at Penfui and the roads of Kupang. Three days later allied reinforcements left Port Darwin for the island, but on the 16th they were attacked by Japanese aircraft and though they suffered no losses, they were ordered back to Darwin! In view of the existing situation the convoy would leave again when the allies had air superiority, but this meant no more troops for Timor.

On February 17th the Japanese troops, intended for the occupation of Timor, embarked at Ambon. Three days later the island had to be attacked. On the 19th the Japanese safeguarded their left flank when they bombed Port Darwin with all the available aircraft from the base Kendari. Assistance was given by aircraft from four carriers—the *Akagi, Kaga, Soryu* and *Hiryu,* which had 36 fighters on board, 71 bombers and 81 attack aircraft—situated in a position about 220 miles north-west of Port Darwin.

On the 20th the Japanese landed according to plan at Dilly and south of Kupang while 307 paratroopers were dropped near the airfield at Penfui. They belonged to the Yokosuka 3rd Special Naval Landing Force and had started early in the morning from Kendari airfield. The next day another 323 paratroopers were dropped at the same place. They too had taken off from Kendari airfield and belonged to the same Landing Force as those dropped on the previous day.

Kupang fell on February 20th and the airfield was occupied two days later. At Dilly the opposition by the allied forces was very small. These forces withdrew into the interior

Above: The Netherlands submarine *K XVIII* on the day of her arrival at Surabaya on July 11th, 1935. In the air two Dornier Wal flying boats salute the newcomer to the tropics. On January 23rd, 1942 the boat sank a Japanese troop transport and though she was damaged by depth charges she managed to return to Surabaya. On March 2nd, 1942 she had to be scuttled. In 1944 the Japanese raised her and used her as an Air Warning Picket Hulk. The ship was stationed in the Madura Strait, but was sunk on July 16th, 1945 by the British submarine *Taciturn*.

Below: The Netherlands destroyer *Piet-Hein* with a Fokker C-VIII-W, the V 12, aboard. This type of ship did not carry aircraft when going into action, as neither X nor Y gun could then be used.

Top: A Netherlands destroyer of the Admiral class in tropical waters.

Above: Two Netherlands destroyers at full speed laying a smoke-screen during exercises. On the left is the *Kortenaer,* the first ship to be sunk in the Battle of the Java Sea.

Top right: The cruisers *Java* (left) and *De Ruyter* (right) during gunnery exercises in tropical waters.

Middle right: The Dornier flying boat D 35 in a bay somewhere in the Netherlands East Indies. In the background is a ship of the 'Gouvernementsmarine' (a civil maritime force) *The Valk,* which was sunk as a blockship in the port of Tjilatjap on March 7th, 1942. It was raised in April 1943 by the Japanese and commissioned as Patrol-boat *104* on January 31st, 1944. On August 2nd, 1945 she struck a mine in the Shimonoseki Strait.

Bottom right: Three Netherlands destroyers in line ahead formation.

Above: A view of the deck of the cruiser *Java* during gunnery exercises. Two of the ten 15cm guns in shields can be clearly seen. In the background, half-hidden in the gun smoke, is a Netherlands destroyer.

Top right: Two Dornier Wal flying boats on patrol in the archipelago. Note the different colours in which the aircraft were painted.

Middle right: The Dornier Do-24 K X 19, flying a patrol over part of the Netherlands East Indies. This flying boat was destroyed on January 25th, 1942 during a night landing at Menari, an island in Madura Strait off the mouth of the River Solo. The accident, in which two members of the crew were killed, was the result of pilot exhaustion.

Bottom right: The Dornier Do-24 K flying boat X 1, which was lost together with four other aircraft during an air attack on March 3rd, 1942 on Broome (Australia) by Japanese aircraft.

D39

18

X-1

Below: A Fokker C-XI-W, the W 1, is catapulted off the cruiser *De Ruyter.* The W 1 was destroyed by own personnel when the Netherlands East Indies capitulated.

Bottom: The submarine depot ship *Zuiderkruis.* She managed to reach Trincomalee after she left Tjilatjap on February 28th, 1942. Alongside are from left to right the Netherlands submarines *K XII, K XIV, K XVII, K XV* and *K XI.* The *K XVII* was last seen on December 16th, 1941 off Tingga Island. She was probably sunk by Japanese ships or ran into a minefield in position 03 40 North 104 35 East.

Top: The cruiser *Java* at anchor.

Above: The British cruiser *Exeter.* In December 1939 she fought a gallant battle together with the *Ajax* and *Achilles* against the German *Graf Spee* off the Rio de la Plata.

Below: The minelayer *Prins van Oranje* which was stationed at Tarakan when the Japanese invasion of the Netherlands East Indies started. She was sunk by two Japanese ships while trying to escape.

Top left: General Sir Archibald Wavell, Supreme Commander of the South-West Pacific Area (ABDA-area).

Bottom left: The arrival of General Wavell on January 10th, 1942 at Kemajoran airfield near Batavia. Third from the left is Vice-Admiral C. E. L. Helfrich, fourth from the left is General Sir Archibald Wavell, sixth from the left is Lt-Gen H. ter Poorten.

Above: The first conference of the ABDA-command at the home of the Commander-in-Chief of the Royal Netherlands Navy in the Netherlands East Indies in Batavia on the afternoon of January 10th, 1942. Standing is Lt Cdr A. H. W. von Freijtag Drabbe, aide-de-camp to the Commander-in-Chief. Anti-clockwise are seated: Col Kengen (Army Air Force of the Royal Netherlands East Indies Army); Lt-Col Mantel (Royal Netherlands East Indies Army); Lt-Gen H. ter Poorten (Commander-in-Chief Royal Netherlands East Indies Army); Rear-Admiral W. R. Purnell USN; Admiral T. C. Hart USN; Vice-Admiral C. E. L. Helfrich RNLN (Commander-in-Chief Royal Netherlands Navy in the Netherlands East Indies); Vice-Admiral Sir Geoffrey Layton; Rear-Admiral A. F. E. Palliser (not visible); Rear-Admiral J. J. A. van Staveren RNLN (not visible); Air-Marshal Sir Charles Burnett RAAF (seen at the back); Air-Cdre J. E. Hewitt RAAF; Maj-Gen L. H. Brereton USAF (not visible); Lt-Gen H. G. Brett (US Army); Gen Sir Archibald Wavell (Supreme Commander ABDA-area); Lt-Gen Sir Henry Pownall (Chief of Staff); Grp Capt L. Darval RAF.

Far top left: Admiral T. C. Hart USN, Commander of the Naval Forces in the ABDA-area from January 15th to February 14th, 1942 (ABDA-float).

Top left: A photograph of Karel Doorman when, as a lieutenant, he was at Soesterberg to receive his wings.

Bottom left: During the bombing of the Striking Force on February 4th, 1942 near Kangean the American cruiser *Marblehead* received a hit which killed 15 men. The ship entered the port of Tjilatjap on February 6th to repair the damage. The men who had lost their lives were buried here. The *Marblehead* survived the war and was scrapped on February 27th, 1946.

Top: The American destroyer *Pillsbury*, which took part in the action of the Badung Strait. She was sunk on March 1st, 1942 by a Japanese naval force which operated in the Indian Ocean to prevent the evacuation of personnel and material from Tjilatjap, on the south coast of Java, to Australia or Ceylon.

Above: A Japanese convoy steaming to the south.

Right: Vice-Admiral C. E. L. Helfrich RNLN, Commander-in-Chief of the Royal Netherlands Navy in the Netherlands East Indies; from February 14th to 25th, 1942 he was Commander of the Naval Forces in the ABDA-area (ABDA-float).

Below: The American cruiser *Houston.* When the news of the loss of this ship reached the United States, which was almost nine months later (!), many people from the city of Houston volunteered to be a member of the crew of the new cruiser *Houston.* This cruiser was originally named *Vicksburg,* but was renamed *Houston* on October 12th, 1942.

Below: A Dornier Do-24 K flying boat on an auxiliary airbase somewhere in the Netherlands East Indies. In total there were 43 of such bases spread in the archipelago. The usefulness of these bases depended on the prevailing weather conditions. Their task was to enable the crew to take some rest and to carry out some minor repairs on the aircraft.

Bottom: Rear-Admiral K. W. F. M. Doorman, during an official reception, in a conversation with Dr H. J. van Mook, Director of Economic Affairs of the Netherlands East Indies Government. Van Mook led the Netherlands economic delegation during the talks with the Japanese in the years 1940 and 1941.

Top left: The sinking of the *Van Ghent* after she had struck a reef in Gaspar Strait on February 15th, 1942.

Middle left: The British cruiser *Exeter* manages to evade some Japanese bombs during the Battle of Gaspar Strait.

Bottom left: A photograph taken during the bombardment of the Striking Force in Gaspar Strait on February 15th, 1942. On the right is the flagship of Rear-Admiral K. W. F. M. Doorman, on the left a destroyer of the Admiral class and in the middle the *Tromp*.

Below: The American 'four-stacker' *John D. Ford*, one of the many American ships which fought in Netherlands Indies waters against superior Japanese forces. The ship managed to escape from the Indies and survived the war. Fifty sisterships were handed over to the Royal Navy in 1940 and 'saved the world'.

Bottom: A view of the Dornier Do-24, K, X 17, which was shot down during an air battle near Noordwachter. The X 18 was also brought down in this encounter.

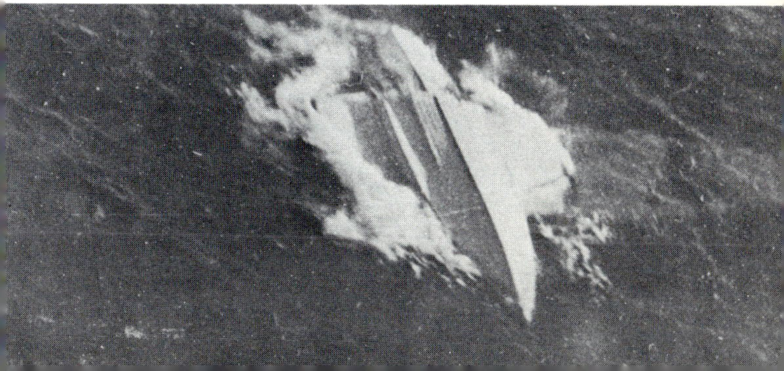

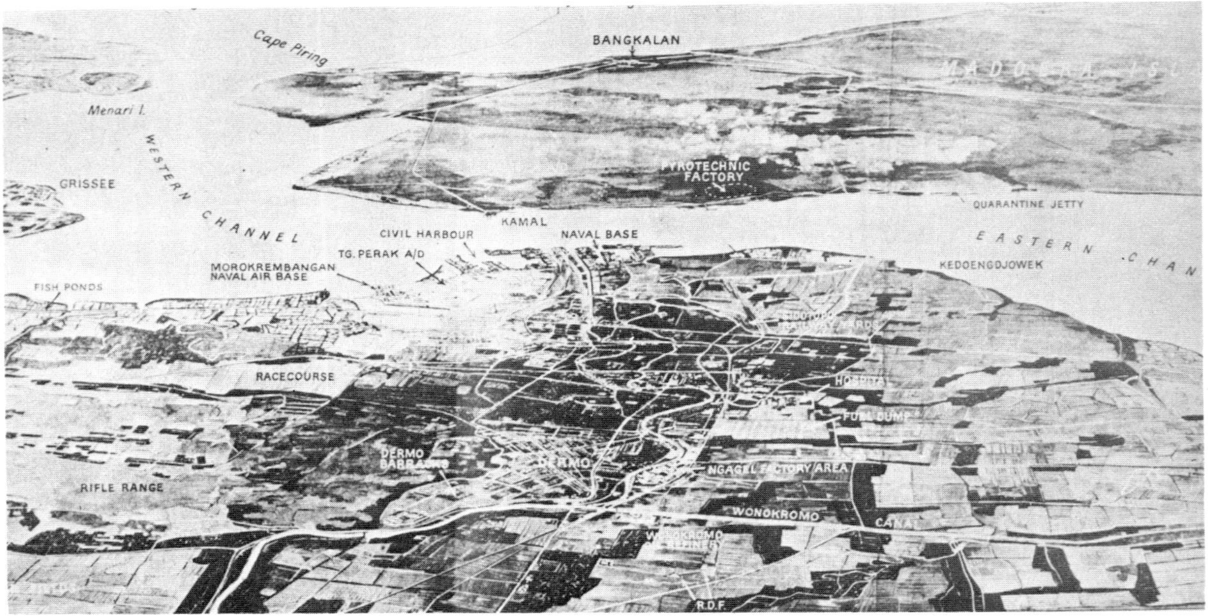

An oblique view of Surabaya, showing the approaches to the port and the position of the various harbours and airfields.

and for nearly a year waged a successful guerrilla war against the invaders.

The next Japanese step, Bali, also proceeded without a hitch. The troops earmarked for this operation were the Kanamura Detachment of the 48th Army Division. They had left Lingayen Gulf on February 5th and via Jolo arrived at Menado on the 15th. On the 18th they left in two transports for the east coast of Bali. The same day the ships anchored at the appointed place near Sanur and the troops went ashore without meeting any resistance.

On February 19th Den Passar airfield was captured by the Japanese in the afternoon. With the fall of Bali the air route between Australia and the Netherlands Indies had been completely cut. On the night of February 24th a second Japanese group consisting of six transports anchored off Sanur and landed the remainder of the forces.

Action of the Striking Force against the Japanese in the waters of Bali.

"This resolute Dutchman (Admiral Helfrich) never abandoned hope, and continued to attack the enemy vigorously regardless of cost or the overwhelming strength opposed to him." *(Winston S. Churchill)*

ABDA-float decided to use the Striking Force against the Japanese invasion fleet at Bali. After the raid through the Gaspar Strait this fleet was, however, dispersed. The *De Ruyter*, *Exeter*, *Hobart*, *Barker* and *Bulmer* were at Tandjong Priok on February 16th; the *Java*, *Tromp*, *Piet Hein*, *Kortenaer*, *Edwards* and *Parrott* first sailed to Oosthaven and from there to Tandjong Priok.

It was necessary to regroup the ships and originally it was planned to concentrate them on Surabaya, but the speed of the Japanese advance on Bali was so great that a new plan had to be made.

One group of the Striking Force was to assemble in Tjilatjap and make the first attack on the Japanese fleet at about 21.30hrs on February 19th; a second group was to leave Surabaya to attack about four hours later. A third group was formed by motor torpedo boats which were ordered to attack the Japanese after the Striking Force.

According to plan the first Attack Group, consisting of the *De Ruyter, Java, Piet Hein, Ford* and *Pope*, went on the run in line-ahead formation on February 19th at about 21.30hrs. The cruiser sailed well ahead of the destroyers. About an hour later the *Java* opened fire and completely surprised the Japanese. It was noticed that one Japanese destroyer was hit several times by gunfire. Shortly afterwards the three allied destroyers had a hot reception from the Japanese, who by now were ready for the next engagement. In the course of this fight the *Piet Hein* received a hit in the engine-room and came to a stop. A fire broke out. The ship was hit again and again by two Japanese destroyers, the *Oshio* and *Asashio*, and also received one or more torpedo hits. She finally sank. *Ford* and *Pope* were now on their own. They launched their torpedoes and after about five minutes the engagement was broken off. No results could be reported.

The second Attack Group, consisting of the *Tromp, Stewart, Parrott, Edwards* and *Pillsbury*, also kept strictly to schedule. It was planned that the four American destroyers should steam ahead of the *Tromp*. At about 01.30hrs on February 20th the first Japanese ships were sighted to port and directly the American destroyers went in to the attack. During the ensuing action the *Stewart* was hit aft, damaging the steering engine. Meanwhile the *Tromp* had come up and engaged Japanese ships on her starboard side. The Dutch light cruiser was hit 11 times, which caused damage on the bridge and control tower. During this second action one Japanese destroyer, the *Michishio*, was badly damaged by torpedoes, which were probably fired by the *Pillsbury*, and had to be towed to Makassar. After the allied ships had withdrawn to the north the scene was set for the third Attack Group, the motor torpedo boats. In two groups of four boats each—an eastern and western group—the boats came on the scene of battle. Actually nine motor torpedo boats had left Surabaya, but ten minutes after their departure, one had to return to harbour after she had hit a lightbuoy. Only the first group saw a target, went in to the attack but they were not able to launch their torpedoes. At daybreak the boats retired to the depot ship *Krakatau* anchored in a bay on the south coast of Java.

The Battle of Badung Strait was over; the results were disappointing. For the loss of one destroyer and damage to a light cruiser and a destroyer the allies had managed to damage only three Japanese destroyers, the *Oshio, Michishio* and *Asashio*, and one transport, the *Sagami Maru* (7,189brt), which was damaged by allied air attacks on February 19th while—together with the second transport, the *Sasako Maru* (9,258brt)—she was unloading troops and material for the occupation of Bali. The *Tromp* had to be sent to Australia for repairs.

The Gap in the Malay Barrier is Closed

"These fellows mean to fight. We will have to be prepared." *(Secretary of State Cordell Hull)*

Java now lay wide open to the Japanese. As mentioned before they had started to bomb Surabaya soon after the occupation of Kendari, since when it was attacked practically every day, causing considerable damage.

The Japanese had planned to attack Java from the west and east. The main part of the Western Expeditionary Force was to land in Bantam Bay, while smaller groups would land at Merak and Eretam Wetan. The Eastern Expeditionary Force would land near Kragan. From incomplete reconnaissance messages the allies had deduced these Japanese intentions.

On February 18th the invasion fleet for Western Java left Camranh Bay, a day later followed by the Eastern invasion fleet, which departed from Jolo. Both landings were scheduled to take place on February 28th. On February 21st Admiral Helfrich had split up the Striking Force in a Western Striking Force under command of Commodore J. A. Collins RAN, based at Tandjong Priok, and an Eastern Striking Force under command of Rear-Admiral K. W. F. M. Doorman, based at Surabaya, so as to be able to meet any Japanese attacks on Java. The Western Striking Force consisted of the *Exeter, Hobart, Dragon, Danae, Electra, Jupiter, Scout* and *Tenedos*, while the *Perth* arrived on February 24th. The Eastern Striking Force consisted of the *De Ruyter, Java, Houston, Witte de With, Banckert, Kortenaer, Paul Jones* and *Alden*.

If the situation became critical the two forces could be united again into a Combined Striking Force. However, this decision was delayed until the last moment because of fuel shortage and Admiral Helfrich therefore wanted to fuel the ships as long as possible at these places.

On February 25th allied submarines—*Truant, S 37, S 38, O 19, K VIII* and *K X*—were stationed on the approach routes which the Japanese forces might follow. On this same day the Eastern invasion fleet was sighted by a Dutch Catalina. Upon receipt of the signal Admiral Helfrich decided to concentrate the surface ships in the east, as it was thought that the expeditionary force for this area might land before the Western Expeditionary Force. Two cruisers and three destroyers—the *Exeter, Perth, Electra, Encounter* and *Jupiter*—steamed from Tandjong Priok to Surabaya. Also on February 25th some Japanese troops landed on Bawean Island from a motor schooner; they carried wireless sets with them. As has been related before, this same day witnessed the dissolution of ABDA-command. Furthermore two important messages were received on the 25th. One was from MacArthur and reported the presence of a large concentration of ships at Jolo on February 20th. The second message was sent on the 24th by a reconnaissance plane, which had carried out a reconnoitring patrol to Makassar Strait. She reported a transport fleet on a southerly course. It was her last message before she was intercepted and shot down.

CHAPTER TWO

The Battle

Prelude to the Battle of the Java Sea

"You must continue attacks till the enemy is destroyed." *(Admiral Helfrich's orders to Admiral Doorman)*

For several nights Doorman cruised with his force off the north coast of Java and Madura to prevent any unexpected landings of Japanese troops. On February 26th the reinforcements arrived in the roads of Surabaya. That same day Admiral Doorman held his last conference with the commanding officers of the Combined Striking Force and their staff officers. It was decided to sail again that evening.

There was a slight chance that some cover from aircraft could be expected, but any hope of this was soon dashed. The small carrier *Langley* was underway to Tjilatjap with 32 P-40 fighters on board, but unfortunately she was sunk by Japanese aircraft on February 27th, about 50 miles south of Tjilatjap.

On the 26th the remaining ships of the Western Striking Force made a patrol in the direction of Banka Strait in pursuance of a message from an aircraft of the Royal Air Force which had reported an invasion fleet about 100 miles north of this passage. Nothing was sighted, however, and after reporting back at Tandjong Priok the next day the ships were ordered to Ceylon.

At about 18.30hrs Doorman and his ships left the port of Surabaya and set course for the Java Sea. During the coming night he made a sweep along the north coast of Madura as far as Sapudi Strait and then back to Tuban. No contact with any Japanese forces was made. It has been argued that the commander of the Combined Striking Force could have carried out a sweep to the north and thus have

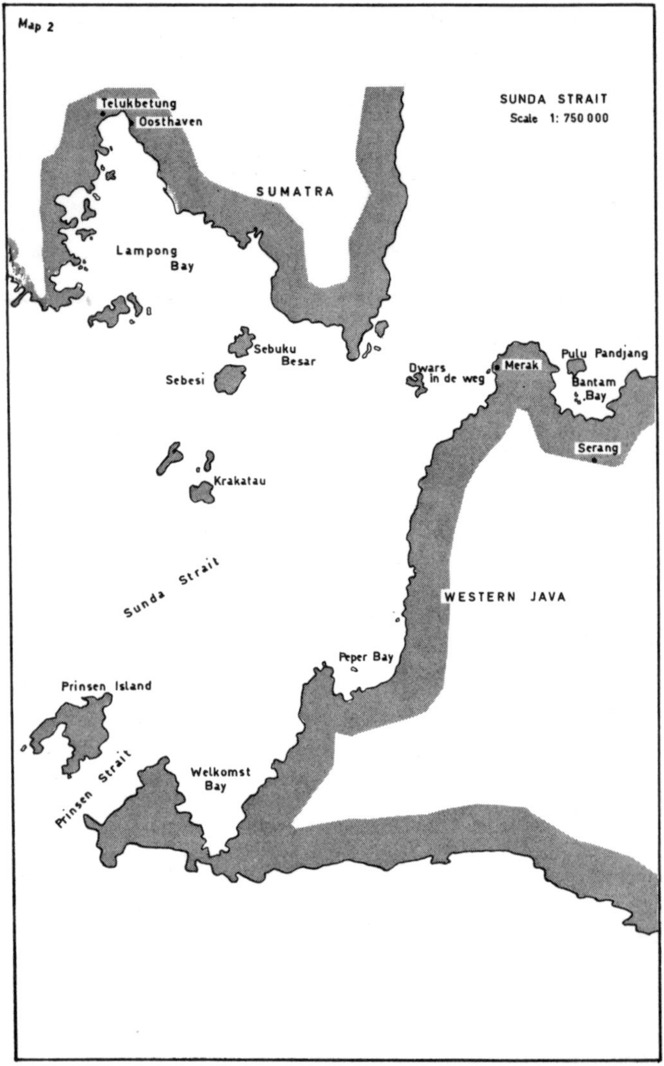
Map 2
SUNDA STRAIT
Scale 1: 750 000
Telukbetung
Oosthaven
SUMATRA
Lampong
Bay
Sebuku
Besar
Sebesi
Dwars
in de weg
Merak
Pulu Pandjang
Bantam
Bay
Serang
Krakatau
Sunda Strait
WESTERN JAVA
Peper Bay
Prinsen Island
Prinsen Strait
Welkomst
Bay

approached the Japanese invasion fleet, but Doorman was probably convinced that the landings would take place that night. By steering a northerly course, therefore, he might have missed the Japanese fleet and arrived too late at the landing beaches.

The Naval Commander Surabaya had made a request to the American air force at Malang for some Liberator aircraft with naval observers so that the necessary assistance to the Combined Striking Force could be given. The American commanding officer agreed to this plan, but ABDA-air at Bandung ordered a different mission to be carried out and gave the order to evacuate. In the meantime on February 21st a patrol had been instituted in the coastal waters from Tandjong Priok to the south of Sunda Strait in order to watch for possible Japanese infiltration on to the west coast of Java, while on this same day Admiral Helfrich had taken the necessary steps to station submarines on the approach routes of the Japanese invasion fleets. There was, however, one great difficulty; naval headquarters did not know the exact location of the American boats, one of which took a shot at the Japanese forces who had landed on Bawean. The Americans, however, did not really agree with these measures for two reasons: it was very difficult to attack ships hugging the coast and the allies would lose some reconnaissance possibilities! During the past days the Japanese had bombarded cities like Surabaya, Malang, Madiun, Kalidjati, Semarang, Batavia and other places while at the same time attacks were carried out on the various airfields, whereby many valuable allied aircraft were lost. During the bombardment of Surabaya a floating dock carrying the American destroyer *Stewart* capsized and the American ship was badly damaged. Three days later the *Banckert* received heavy damage under similar circumstances from a near miss, in the port of Surabaya.

Friday, February 27th, 1942

"He, who in time of peace, wants to enjoy the advantages that the navy offers, must in time of war in all honesty honour the bill." *(The commander of the Netherlands naval squadron in the East Indies in 1912)*

After Doorman's search along part of the north coast of

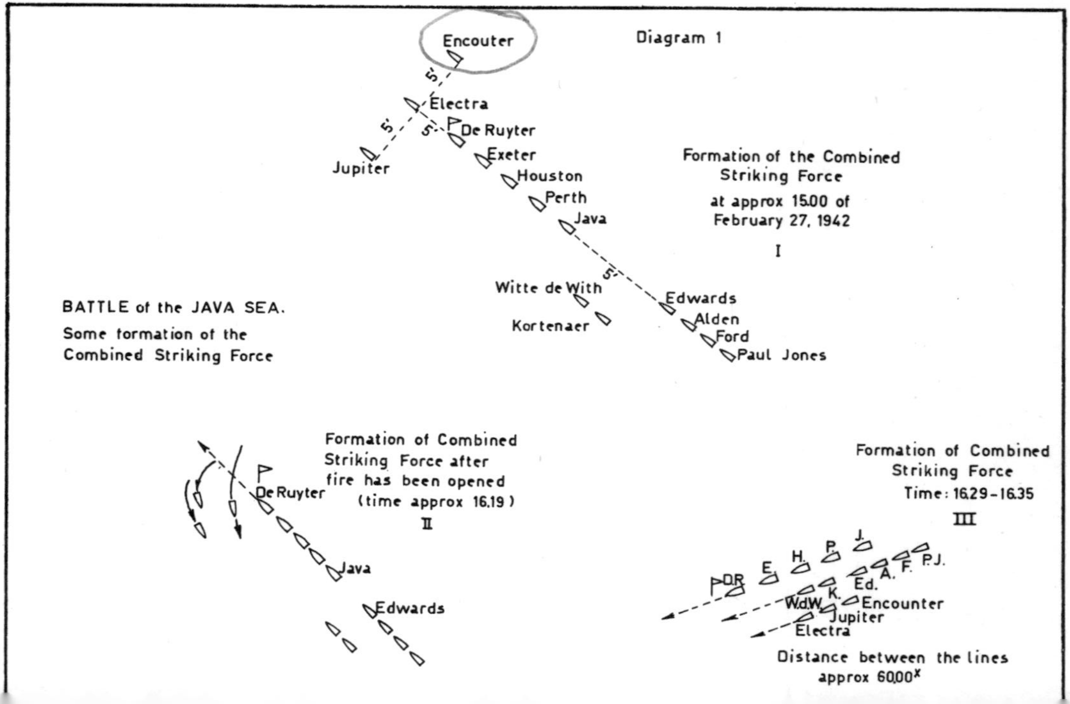

Diagram 1
BATTLE of the JAVA SEA.
Some formation of the
Combined Striking Force
Encouter
Electra
De Ruyter
Jupiter
Exeter
Houston
Perth
Java
Witte de With
Kortenaer
Edwards
Alden
Ford
Paul Jones
5'
Formation of the Combined
Striking Force
at approx 15.00 of
February 27, 1942
I
Formation of Combined
Striking Force after
fire has been opened
(time approx 16.19)
II
De Ruyter
Java
Edwards
Formation of Combined
Striking Force
Time: 16.29–16.35
III
D.R. E. H. P. J.
W.d.W. K. Ed. A. F. P.J.
Encounter
Jupiter
Electra
Distance between the lines
approx 60,00x

Formation of Combined Striking Force at 16.52

IV

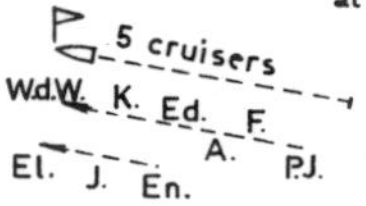

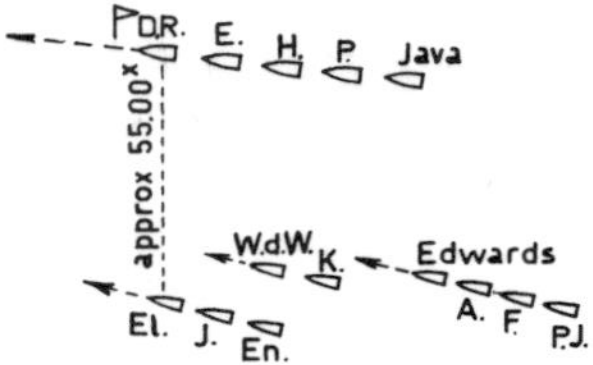

Formation of Combined Striking Force at 17.07

V

Formation and movements of Combined Striking Force in the period of 17.08 – 17.40

Scale 1 : 200.000

VI

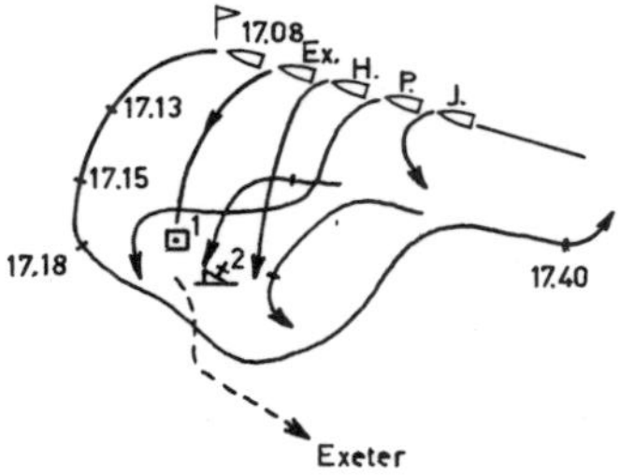

1. Exeter was hit by an 8"shell at about 17.07 and came to a stop(⊡) at 17.14
2. Kortenaer was hit by a torpedo at 17.13 and sank at 17.15

East Java and Madura during the night of February 26th and early morning of the 27th, the Combined Striking Force approached the entrance of the Westervaarwater at about noon on the 27th and steamed on to Surabaya to refuel.

At 14.27hrs Doorman received the news he had been waiting for: the invasion fleet had been sighted near Bawean. Without hesitation he turned about with his ships and set course for the Japanese fleet. This was one of the few occasions when a reconnaissance signal was received aboard the flagship without any delay. It was transmitted by a Dutch Catalina at 13.50hrs.

The Combined Striking Force consisted of the following ships: the cruisers *De Ruyter* (flag), *Java*, *Exeter*, *Houston* and *Perth*, and the destroyers *Electra*, *Encounter*, *Jupiter*, *Kortenaer*, *Witte de With*, *Alden*, *John D. Edwards*, *John D. Ford* and *Paul Jones;* a total of two heavy cruisers, three light cruisers and nine destroyers (for the various formations during the battle see Diagram 1).

The Japanese naval forces were those of the Eastern Invasion Force consisting of 41 transports under the command of Rear-Admiral Nishimura on board his flagship *Naka*. They were covered by a large force under Rear-Admiral Takagi flying his flag on the *Nachi*. On February 26th the Japanese had split this force in two groups so that the next day one group was north-west of Bawean and one west of the island. They no longer expected to meet with much allied resistance and were therefore taken by surprise when their reconnaissance aircraft reported at about 10.20hrs the presence of the Combined Striking Force. Takagi was at pains to effect the necessary concentration of forces in time; he had under his command two heavy cruisers, two light cruisers and 14 destroyers.

They were:

Naka (flag)		4th Destroyer Flotilla
Asagumo (flag)	9th Destroyer Division	
Minegumo		
Murasame (flag)	2nd Destroyer Division	
Samidare		
Harusame		
Yudachi		

Ship	Division	Flotilla
Jintsu (flag)		2nd Destroyer Flotilla
Yukikaze (flag)	16th Destroyer Division	2nd Destroyer Flotilla
Amatsukaze	16th Destroyer Division	2nd Destroyer Flotilla
Tokitsukaze	16th Destroyer Division	2nd Destroyer Flotilla
Hatsukaze	16th Destroyer Division	2nd Destroyer Flotilla
Yamakaze (flag)	24th Destroyer Division	2nd Destroyer Flotilla
Kawakaze	24th Destroyer Division	2nd Destroyer Flotilla

These ships formed the convoy escort, while close support was given by

Nachi (flag)	5th Cruiser Division
Haguro	5th Cruiser Division
Ushio (flag)	7th Destroyer Division
Sazanami	7th Destroyer Division

During the battle of the Java Sea the 7th Destroyer Division was incorporated in the 2nd Destroyer Flotilla. The destroyers *Natsugumo* (9th Destroyer Division) and *Umikaze* (24th Destroyer Division) remained with the convoy and did not take part in the Battle (for a comparison of the two fleets see Table 7). There has been some confusion about the number of destroyers, but Japanese sources indicate that there were 14.

Numerically the Japanese did not have much advantage, but in all other respects they were superior. Doorman's communications were weak, he had no aircraft to carry out reconnaissances—something which the Japanese were doing continuously—and his personnel were tired. To illustrate this, mention can be made of a report by Doorman to Helfrich shortly after noon to say that the limit of endurance of his personnel had been reached and would soon be exceeded. Nevertheless, morale was very high. When the ships left harbour on the 26th there was not one man aboard who did not realise what lay ahead. And yet everyone returned to his ship on time! Very important too was the fact that the ships had never worked together before, the *Perth* for instance did not arrive at Tandjong Priok until February 24th.

Furthermore, the Japanese had one weapon of which the allies knew nothing, the 60.9cm (24in) torpedo, Type 93, which had an extremely long running distance. These so-called Long Lance torpedoes could run 22,000yds at 49 knots; 35,000yds at 40 knots and 44,000yds at 36 knots. They ran on a liquid oxygen propellant and left very little track. The western world should really have been informed of this new development in the torpedo-arm, for as early as 1937 the *Weyers Taschenbuch der Kriegsflotten* made mention of a torpedo of 60.9cm, which was being installed in the Harusame-class destroyers!

The Commanders

"Admiral Doorman's leadership was excellent." *(Captain O. L. Gordon RN, commanding officer of HMS* Exeter*)*

The two commanders, who were to oppose each other in mortal combat, were Rear-Admiral K. W. F. M. Doorman, commander of the Combined Striking Force, and Rear-Admiral T. Takagi, commander of the 5th Cruiser Division and in tactical command over all the Japanese ships during the Battle of the Java Sea.

Karel Willem Frederik Marie Doorman was born on April 23rd, 1889 at Utrecht and entered the Royal Netherlands Naval College in Den Helder at the age of 17. On August 24th, 1910 he became an officer and after serving on various ships, in the Far East as well as in the Netherlands, he went in August 1915 to the air division of the navy at Soesterberg. In 1921 he attended a staff-course at the naval staff-college in The Hague. Then there followed several postings; at the naval department in Batavia; on board the armoured ship De Zeven Provincien and on the naval staff in The Hague. He served as a commanding officer on board destroyers and cruisers.

From August 17th, 1938 until May 16th, 1940 he was in command of the Royal Netherlands Naval Air Service in the East Indies, while on the latter date he was promoted to the rank of Rear-Admiral and appointed commander of the Netherlands Squadron in the East. Considering Doorman had earned his wings as a young officer and had a very close connection with the naval air service he can undoubtedly be qualified as being "air-minded" and he must have been aware of the importance of an adequate air reconnaissance. Doorman was always asking for assistance from aircraft and during the last staff conference, on February 26th, he told the Naval Commander Surabaya that he sincerely hoped he could rely on the necessary information and assistance from the air. Fate would have it otherwise; there were just no aircraft available. Furthermore the aeroplane from the *Houston* was left behind in Surabaya as one prepared for a night action. Doorman was a very special and very difficult man not only to others but also to himself. He had a tropical illness which sometimes caused him much inconvenience, and which would not have made it easier for him to carry the weighty responsibility of uniting a Striking Force, which moreover changed its formation several times. Yet it was his leadership and stubborn determination which nevertheless made this Striking Force an effective force. When the flagship was fatally hit by a Japanese torpedo Doorman and his staff could have left the ship, as there was sufficient time to get into the boats, but instead he chose to go under with the *De Ruyter*.

Takeo Takagi was born on January 25th, 1892 at Fukushima and when 16 years old he went to the naval college on the island of Etajima, near Hiroshima. After four years he was appointed an officer. At the age of 23 Takagi went into the submarine service, in which he served for 13 years and finished as the commanding officer of the most modern submarines of his day. He then attended various staff-courses and received postings abroad on board ships as captain, and on task forces as staff-officer. On November 15th, 1938 he was promoted to the rank of Rear-Admiral, and nearly three years later, on September 6th, 1941, he was appointed Commander of the 5th Cruiser Division.

Thus on February 27th, 1942 two men were opposing each other, each of whom had had a successful career to date. One was especially acquainted with the air aspect of naval warfare, the other had spent many years in submarines. It was ironic when it came to the point of hard and ruthless reality that the former had, with one or two exceptions, no aircraft at his disposal, while the latter had complete air support!

The Battle of the Java Sea—Day Action

"All ships—follow me." *(Admiral Doorman's signal of 18.00hrs during the Battle of the Java Sea)*

After the ships had reversed course at about 14.30hrs and had passed through the minefield north of Surabaya at 15.00hrs, they sped off to the north-west. About half an hour later a Japanese aircraft appeared over the allied fleet and dropped some bombs. The ships dispersed, but had re-formed by about 15.50hrs. The course was 315 , speed 24 knots.

There was an easterly wind, force 4. Ten minutes later Admiral Doorman asked for protection from fighter aircraft, but this proved to be impossible as they were needed to accompany three divebombers, which had to carry out an attack on the Japanese transport fleet. ABDA-air had conceived this plan, but omitted to inform ABDA-float!

At 16.12hrs *Electra,* steaming in the van, sighted the first Japanese ships and signalled: "One cruiser, unknown number large destroyers, bearing 330 degrees, speed 18, course 220 degrees." Four minutes later this cruiser, the *Jintsu,* opened fire on the *Electra* at a distance of 18,000 yards, while at the same time the *Electra* and the *Jupiter* fired at the *Jintsu*. Meanwhile the Japanese heavy cruisers *Nachi* and *Haguro* had appeared over the horizon and at 16.17hrs the *Nachi* opened fire. The *Jintsu* and her eight destroyers were trying to take up a favourable position for a torpedo attack. Doorman found himself in a tactical situation which was rapidly deteriorating, because there was the danger that the Japanese would cross the T. He therefore changed course 20 degrees to port.

The distance between the two fleets decreased, so that the allied light cruisers were soon able to open fire. With their superior speed the Japanese destroyers were still heading into a more favourable position to launch their torpedoes, which forced Doorman to make yet another alteration of course to port. The allied ships could not steam faster than 27 knots, this being the maximum speed of the *Kortenaer,* which was the result of boiler difficulties.

The gunnery duel continued with undiminished intensity and though the flagship was twice hit the ship did not suffer any damage as the projectiles did not explode. The *Exeter* and *Houston* also received hits, though here too the damage was not serious. On board the allied ships it had been observed that the Japanese ships had also been hit, but the results must have been negligible as no mention of it is made in their battle reports.

Gradually the allied ships changed course again towards the Japanese fleet, but at 17.05hrs the *Exeter* received a near hit or an underwater hit, from which the ship was slightly damaged. It may even have been a torpedo which did not explode. Shortly afterwards the *Houston* was hit by a shell which did not burst, though the ship had to decrease speed for a few moments. This caused some confusion in the allied formation; the ships began to open out and one or two even started to lay a smoke screen. At 17.08hrs fate struck when the *Exeter* was hit for the second time, which put six of her eight boilers out of action; the cruiser lost speed and turned to port followed by all ships astern of her as they thought that Doorman had ordered a simultaneous alteration of course to the south. *De Ruyter,* however, continued on her course and speed.

Forthwith the *Perth* began to lay a smoke-screen around the stricken cruiser to hide her from the Japanese ships. During the entire action thus far, Japanese aircraft had circled above the Striking Force and had no doubt communicated important information to their ships. Now and then the allied ships took a shot at these spotting planes but this could hardly have impressed them.

The turn to port by the four allied cruisers caused confusion amongst the destroyers which were steaming line ahead on the port beam of the cruiser formation and in this mêlée the *Kortenaer* received a torpedo hit at 17.13hrs. She broke in two and sank within two minutes.

Various ships observed torpedoes rushing through the water and by carrying out avoiding actions caused complete chaos. The explosions of the surfacing torpedoes added an extra element of uncertainty. In a Japanese report, the so-called Chikaya report, it is said that in the battle area

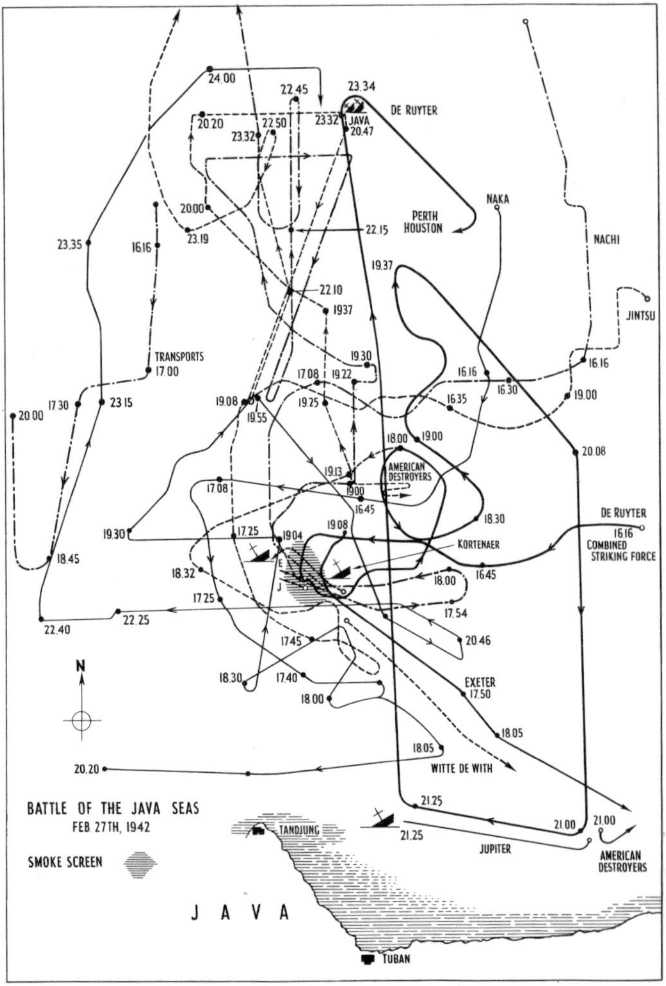
BATTLE OF THE JAVA SEAS
FEB. 27TH, 1942
SMOKE SCREEN
N
DE RUYTER
JAVA
PERTH
HOUSTON
NAKA
NACHI
JINTSU
TRANSPORTS
AMERICAN DESTROYERS
KORTENAER
DE RUYTER
COMBINED STRIKING FORCE
EXETER
WITTE DE WITH
JUPITER
AMERICAN DESTROYERS
TANDJUNG
J A V A
TUBAN
24.00
22.45
23.34
20.20
22.50
23.32
23.32
20.47
20.00
23.19
22.15
23.35
16.16
19.37
22.10
1937
19.30
17.08
19.22
16.16
16.30
16.16
17.00
17.30
23.15
20.00
19.08
19.55
19.25
16.35
19.00
18.00
19.00
20.08
19.13
1900
16.45
17.08
18.30
16.16
19.30
17.25
19.04
19.08
18.45
18.32
18.00
16.45
17.25
17.54
22.40
22.25
17.45
20.46
18.30
17.40
17.50
18.00
18.05
18.05
20.20
21.25
21.25
21.00
21.00

explosions were heard, which could have been caused by mines. After studying the battle reports, it was learned that these explosions originated from the oxygen torpedoes. In another Japanese report it is indeed stated that the torpedoes were provided with an automatic detonation mechanism, which operated after the torpedo had reached the end of its run.

It is quite possible that these explosions contributed to Takagi's decision to retreat to the north after the day fight. For he was under the impression that they were caused by mines and one of the considerations for his withdrawal was his fear of entering a minefield. Knowing nothing of the Japanese long-range torpedoes, a few commanding officers thought they were dealing with submarines and the *Witte de With* even launched some depth-charges on a suspected submarine contact. Edwards even sighted a periscope and an official American narrative of this battle says of the torpedoes: "Some were undoubtedly launched by the enemy cruisers and destroyers, but it seems clear that we had come upon an enemy submarine group too."

As for the torpedoes which had sunk the *Kortenaer,* the question can be asked where they came from. It is now known that the Japanese had started to launch their torpedoes at 16.33hrs, namely from the *Naka.* Two minutes later the *Jintsu* followed, then the destroyers, and at 16.52hrs *Haguro* was the last ship to launch her 'fish' in this first attack. Perhaps it was a torpedo from the *Jintsu* that hit the *Exeter* at 17.05hrs without exploding. In a report of the Japanese 2nd Destroyer Flotilla it is stated that at the time the torpedoes, which were launched at 16.34hrs, could have reached the allied ships, "the second cruiser in the line (*Exeter*) was covered in a white-brown smoke, which belched forth from the ship."

Kortenaer could have been hit by a torpedo launched from the *Haguro* and aimed at the *Houston.* When the Dutch destroyer was hit she was on a southerly course and on the starboard bow of the *Houston* at a distance of approximately 3,000 yards. Until now it has been assumed that the Japanese carried out a second torpedo attack between 17.00 and 17.14hrs. This assumption was based

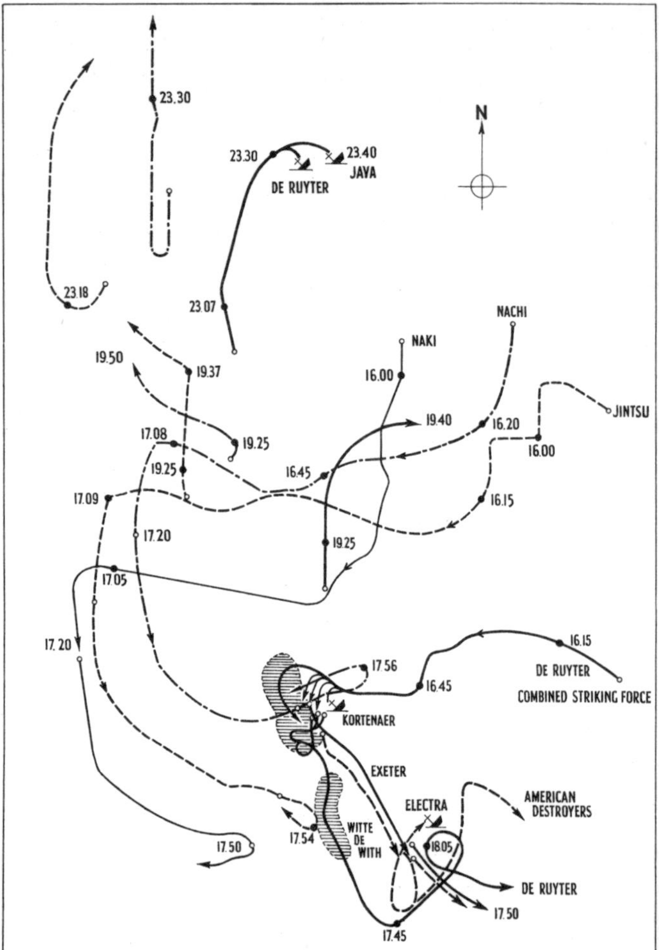

BATTLE OF THE JAVA SEA, FEB. 27TH, 1942

(ACCORDING TO JAPANESE SOURCES)

Diagram 3 SMOKE SCREEN

only on the particulars of the allied torpedo, but in Japanese sources no mention of it is made (see Table 8 for the times that torpedoes were launched). Meanwhile the *De Ruyter* had turned and Admiral Doorman ordered the British destroyers to carry out a counter-attack. This was a difficult task for the ships were widely separated. The area where the action had taken place was now in a state of great confusion, enhanced by the smoke-screen laid to cover the *Exeter*. However, in the end the *Electra* and *Encounter* went into the attack. They plunged through the smoke-screen at about 17.30hrs and came upon the *Jintsu* and her destroyers. The *Jupiter* had also come in contact with the Japanese. It was an unequal fight in which the *Electra* met her doom. At about 18.00hrs she was sunk. The British managed, however, to damage two destroyers; the *Oshio* and *Sazanami*.

At 17.25hrs Doorman was again in control of the situation. The cruisers, with the exception of the *Exeter*, formed up in line ahead, though the sequence had changed slightly. The *De Ruyter* was the first ship in line, followed by the *Perth* and *Houston*, while the *Java* brought up the rear. The four American destroyers followed in the wake of the allied cruisers. The *Exeter* received orders to return to Surabaya, the *Witt de With* as escort. At about the same time Japanese bombers attacked the Combined Striking Force, but fortunately no hits were scored.

At 17.48hrs the Japanese ships began their second torpedo-attack, which was started by the *Haguro* and was completed at 18.07hrs by the *Asagumo*. Just before the latter launched her torpedoes she was hit by gunfire which stopped her for approximately 40 minutes. According to a Japanese damage report the engine room was hit by a shell of a destroyer, while on the port side just above the waterline a few 15cm shells had torn some holes in the hull. After that the *Asagumo* returned to the transport fleet. It is quite possible that the Japanese destroyer was hit by the *Exeter* and *Witt de With*.

Twenty minutes after the Japanese had commenced their torpedo-attack the American destroyers received the order to attack but this was soon revoked and instead Doorman ordered a smoke-screen to be laid to cover the movements of the allied ships.

At 18.00hrs Admiral Doorman made the signal "All ships—follow me" and began to turn away. This signal is often interpreted as "I am going to attack—follow me," but this must be considered incorrect. It was a tactical signal that had to be sent over by signal lamp and because of the prevalent confusion had to be as short as possible. It was also necessary to send a signal which could be sent and understood without difficulty by Dutch and allied signalmen alike. Thus the signal consisted of two parts: the address: "All ships" and the contents: "Follow me".

The Force Commander was going to attempt to locate the transport fleet by a roundabout way and then go into the attack. A quarter of an hour later the fourstackers went into the attack after all, as the senior officer of the division was of the opinion that a torpedo-attack was the most efficient way to cover the retreat. Sunset was at 18.20hrs and shortly afterwards the destroyers launched 24 torpedoes, without success. At about the same time the *Haguro* received a hit by gunfire from one of the allied cruisers probably the *Perth*, which set fire to the catapult aircraft, but the fighting value of the Japanese cruiser was in no way affected, though eye-witnesses later reported that they saw her sinking!

At this very time the Japanese commander, Takagi, also considered it best to retire and he set a course to the north (and not to the west as Doorman was to report at 18.57hrs). Takagi had observed the lighthouse of Surabaya and was afraid that he would run into a minefield or would encounter allied submarines. At about 18.30hrs the American destroyers had rejoined the Combined Striking Force and it was at about this same time that the two fleets lost sight of each other. The Japanese, however, had the advantage of their reconnaissance aircraft which could follow the movements of the allies and report them to their commander. The result of this day action was that the superiority of the Japanese fleet had increased tremendously. The *Kortenaer* and the *Electra* had been sunk; the *Exeter* and the *Witte de With* had returned to Surabaya. The American destroyers had no more torpedoes aboard and were thus really eliminated as fighting units, though they could probably have been used as an anti-submarine screen for they were equipped with Asdic. The fuel problem must, however, be considered as a dominant factor, because it was essential that all destroyers refuel. On the other side, the Japanese had to operate in a second encounter without the *Asagumo*. On both sides the consumption of ammunition had been very high.

The Battle of the Java Sea—Night Action

"I wish to impress upon all of you the necessity for every effort against the enemy to prevent his landing on Java." *(Admiral Doorman in a Fleet Order of February 22nd, 1942)*

At about 18.30hrs there was a lull in the fighting, and during the subsequent hours Doorman tried to discover the position of the convoy. At 18.57hrs he sent the following message to the Commander-in-Chief Netherlands Naval Forces:

"Enemy retreating to the west. Contact broken. Where is the convoy?" It was clear that the commander of the Combined Striking Force was still ignorant of the exact position of the Japanese transport ships, but he was determined, at all costs, to carry out his mission. That he failed ultimately was the result of the Japanese aircraft which continually reported his movements to Takagi, who was thus able to place his ships between the transport fleet and the allied ships. According to an eye-witness the Japanese aircraft would, now and again, drop magnesium flares parallel to the course of the ships. Japanese sources state that there were two aircraft in the air, one from the *Jintsu* and the other from the *Naka*. At about 22.00hrs (about one hour before the next engagement with the allied ships), the aircraft were withdrawn and no further information about the whereabouts of the allied fleet were reported. Doorman was then on a northerly course.

Meanwhile the Naval Commander Surabaya had, on his own initiative, already sent out an aircraft to carry out a reconnaissance. At about 19.00hrs a Catalina of Patwing 10 had taken off from Surabaya and sighted the Combined

Striking Force about 55 minutes later. At 22.22hrs the convoy was indeed found in a position north-west of the island of Bawean, but not until 23.52hrs was this message received by the Naval Commander Surabaya. For Rear-Admiral Doorman it was then too late, because 20 minutes earlier the cruisers *Java* and *De Ruyter* had been fatally hit by Japanese torpedoes.

Initially Doorman had ordered a north-easterly course at about 18.20hrs, but slowly he changed course to the north-west in an attempt to reach the transport fleet behind the escort ships. At 19.27hrs there was a short engagement between the *Jintsu* and three destroyers. Only the *Perth* and *Houston* took part in the gunnery duel that followed. When it was observed that the Japanese ships had launched torpedoes, the ships of the Combined Striking Force turned away individually to starboard. Actually only the *Jintsu* had launched four torpedoes, The Japanese increased speed and withdrew to the north-west while laying a smoke screen. After the allied ships had re-formed, Doorman steamed south-east and at 20.08hrs ordered course to the south. At 21.00hrs the Combined Striking Force reached the 20-metre depth-contour on the north coast of Java and the ships turned to starboard on a westerly course. Scarcely half an hour had elapsed before the force suffered a new set-back. At 21.25hrs the *Jupiter* blew up, came to a stop and sank rapidly.

It is most probable that the destroyer hit a mine, though this can still not be ascertained with absolute certainty. If it was a mine it may have been one in a minefield, which was laid in the night of February 26th/27th, 1942 by the minelayer *Gouden Leeuw* in about 12 metres of water.

By about 21.00hrs the American destroyers had already left the Force and were heading for Surabaya to refuel and to take torpedoes aboard. The Combined Striking Force was thus further weakened; only four cruisers and the *Encounter* remained. And this last destroyer, which could barely keep up with the cruisers, was soon to disappear from the scene of action. At about the time that the *Jupiter* was sunk Doorman had changed course to the north and at 22.00hrs the survivors from the *Kortenaer* were met. The

British destroyer was ordered to pick up these men and then proceed to Surabaya.

The four cruisers steamed on alone to the north and just after 23.00hrs two ships were sighted to port—these turned out to be the *Haguro* and *Nachi*—which were on a southerly course. Both ships immediately turned about and shortly afterwards the guns on both sides opened fire. During this encounter the two Japanese heavy cruisers launched their torpedoes. At 23.32hrs the *Java* was hit by a torpedo; two minutes later the *De Ruyter* received one.

Between 23.50 and 23.55hrs the *Java* sank. About 1½ hours after the flagship was stricken the sea closed over her. It is most likely that the *Java* was torpedoed by the *Nachi,* while the *De Ruyter* was the victim of one of the torpedoes from the *Haguro.*

The *Perth* and the *Houston,* which had nothing to gain by continuing the fight, withdrew from the scene of action and set course for Tandjong Priok at 28 knots. About 60 miles from Tandjong Priok they were discovered by a Japanese reconnaissance aircraft. When dawn broke they received an escort of three Hurricane fighters at the request of *Perth*!

The Continuation of the Battle of the Java Sea—the Battle of Bantam Bay

"When ships and men went down, still fighting, they did not go down in defeat." *(Message of Franklin D. Roosevelt, after the loss of the* Houston, *to Americans from* Houston *who volunteered to replace the lost crew)*

On arrival at Tandjong Priok the ships refuelled and at 14.30hrs received orders to leave after dark for Tjilatjap, a port on the south coast of Java. They had little ammunition on board; the Americans had only 50 shots left per 20.3cm gun; the Australians had even less—20 shots per gun of 15.2cm. Unfortunately they were unable to replenish their supplies. At about 19.30hrs the two ships headed for the open sea and after half an hour they were clear of the minefield outside the harbour. At 16.00hrs on that day a reconnaissance plane had reconnoitred a Japanese convoy consisting of ten ships with an escort. This signal was

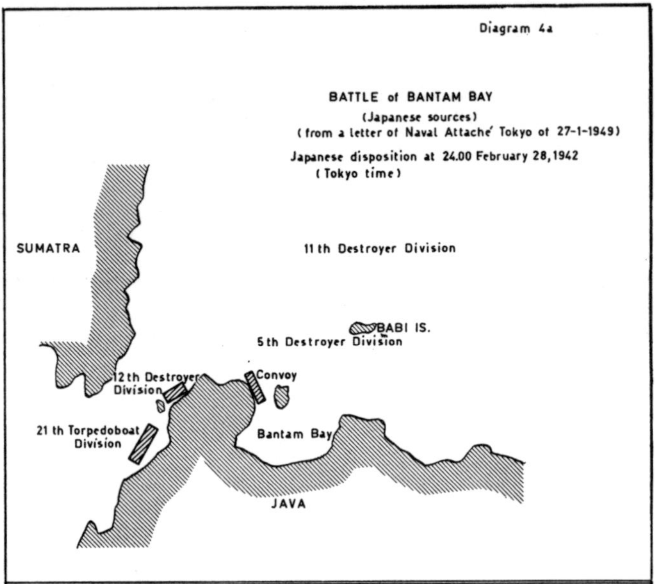
Diagram 4a
BATTLE of BANTAM BAY
(Japanese sources)
(from a letter of Naval Attaché Tokyo of 27-1-1949)
Japanese disposition at 24.00 February 28, 1942
(Tokyo time)
SUMATRA
11 th Destroyer Division
BABI IS.
5 th Destroyer Division
12 th Destroyer Division
Convoy
21 th Torpedoboat Division
Bantam Bay
JAVA

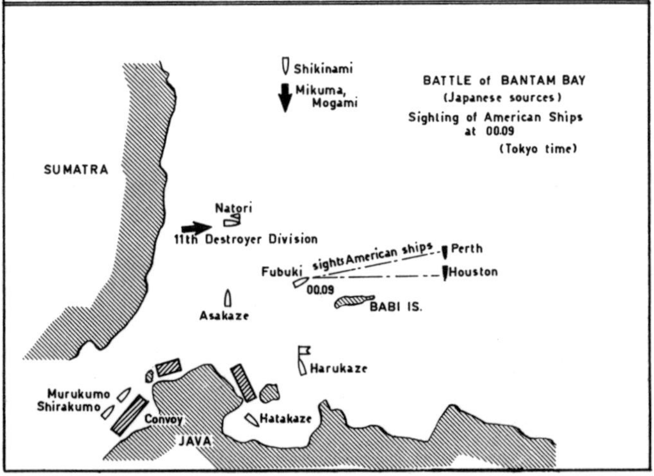
Shikinami
Mikuma, Mogami
BATTLE of BANTAM BAY
(Japanese sources)
Sighting of American Ships at 00.09
(Tokyo time)
SUMATRA
Natori
11th Destroyer Division
sights American ships
Perth
Fubuki
Houston
00.09
Asakaze
BABI IS.
Harukaze
Murukumo
Shirakumo
Convoy
Hatakaze
JAVA

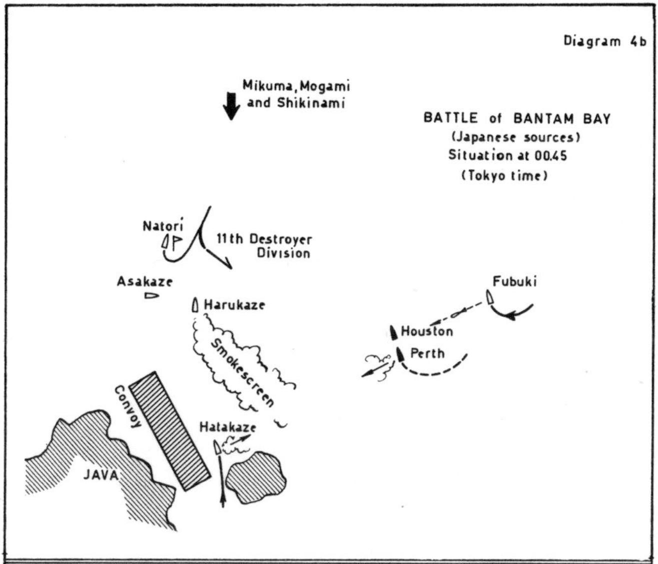
Diagram 4b
Mikuma, Mogami
and Shikinami
BATTLE of BANTAM BAY
(Japanese sources)
Situation at 00.45
(Tokyo time)
Natori
11th Destroyer
Division
Asakaze
Harukaze
Fubuki
Houston
Perth
Smokescreen
Convoy
Hatakaze
JAVA

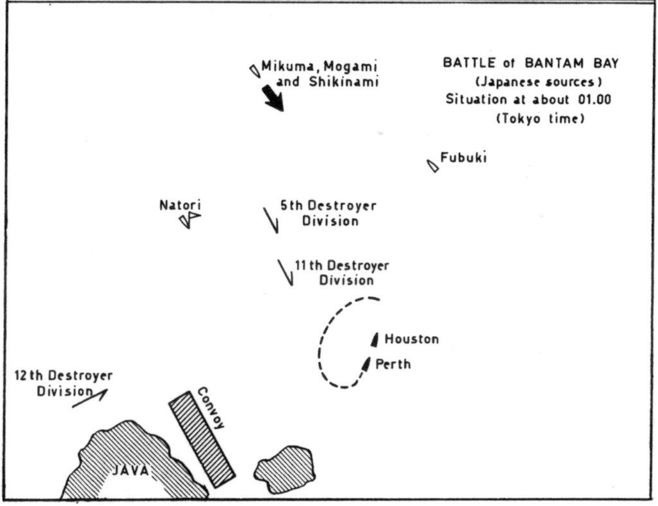
Mikuma, Mogami
and Shikinami
BATTLE of BANTAM BAY
(Japanese sources)
Situation at about 01.00
(Tokyo time)
Fubuki
Natori
5th Destroyer
Division
11th Destroyer
Division
Houston
Perth
12th Destroyer
Division
Convoy
JAVA

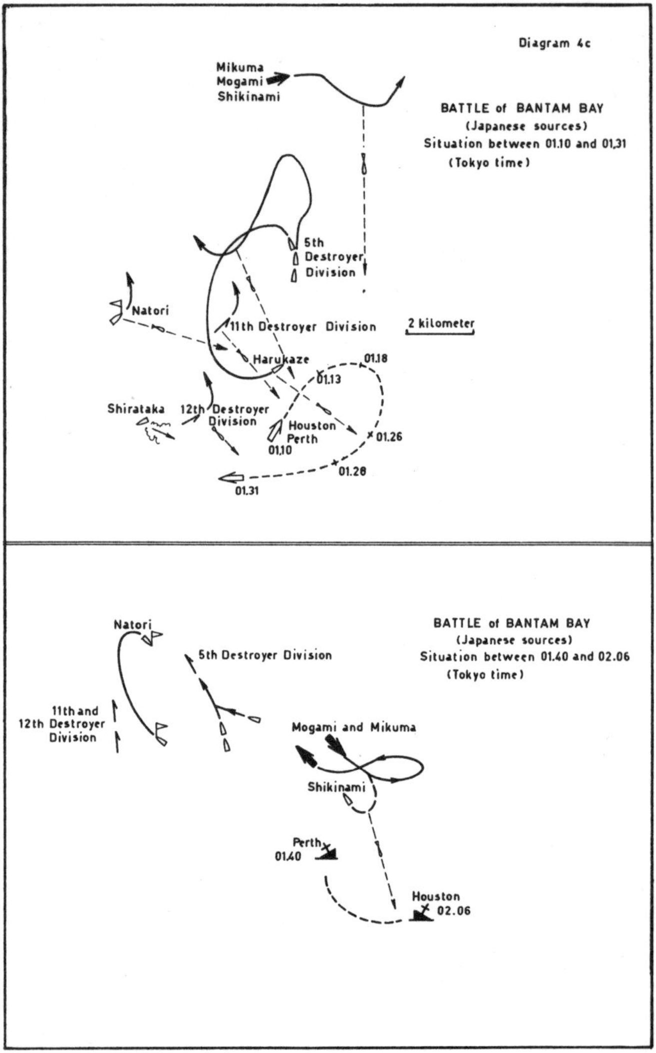

Diagram 4c
Mikuma
Mogami
Shikinami
BATTLE of BANTAM BAY
(Japanese sources)
Situation between 01.10 and 01,31
(Tokyo time)
5th
Destroyer
Division
Natori
11th Destroyer Division
2 kilometer
Harukaze
01.18
01.13
Shirataka
12th Destroyer
Division
Houston
Perth
01,10
01.26
01.28
01.31
BATTLE of BANTAM BAY
(Japanese sources)
Situation between 01.40 and 02.06
(Tokyo time)
Natori
5th Destroyer Division
11th and
12th Destroyer
Division
Mogami and Mikuma
Shikinami
Perth
01.40
Houston
02.06

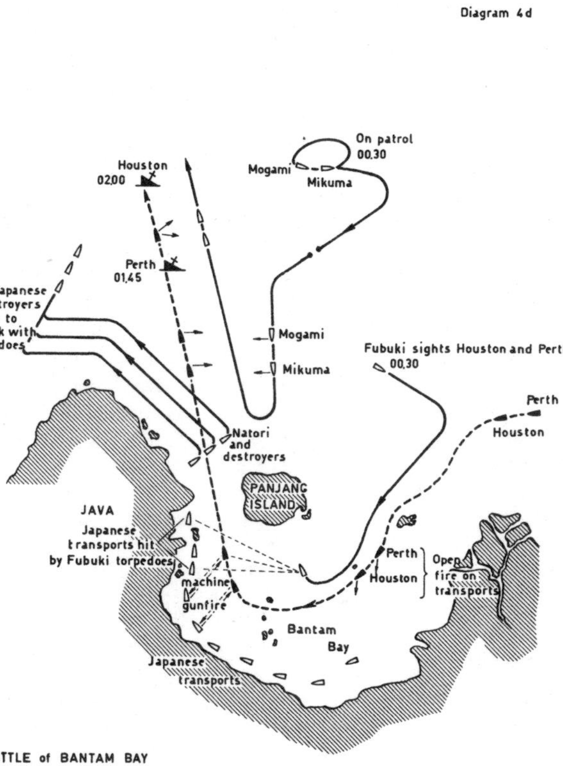

BATTLE of BANTAM BAY

(From a sketch by Rear-Admiral Akira Shoji-See 'Interrogations of Japanese officials', Volume II, page 438).

28 February-1 March 1942

(Tokyo time)

received aboard the *Perth* at 20.00hrs while the allied cruisers set a westerly course.

At 22.39hrs the Japanese destroyer *Fubuki* sighted them near the island of Babi. The Japanese ships were also seen on board the cruisers and it was realised that they had come upon the Western Invasion Force. The situation was ideal to inflict heavy damage on the Japanese, a situation which Doorman had so desperately sought in the past days. Soon after 23.00hrs the two allied cruisers opened fire on the Japanese merchantmen anchored in the Bay of Bantam. At approximately the same time the *Harukaze* started to lay a smoke-screen between the *Perth* and the *Houston* on one side and the anchored ships of the convoy on the other side. It took the Japanese about half an hour before they went into the attack, which consisted also of the launching of torpedoes four of which hit the *Perth* (see Table 9 for the times that torpedoes were launched). The Australian cruiser too had a hard time, because she had been hit by gunfire. But the Japanese were also being hit hard. Just after midnight, at 00.05hrs, the *Perth* was hit by two torpedoes in rapid succession. The ship developed a list to port and sank eight minutes later. The *Houston* had now to stand alone against an overwhelming majority. At 00.20hrs she received three torpedo hits and about 20 minutes later she sank. The Japanese losses consisted of a minesweeper *(W 2)* and a merchantman (*Sakura Maru* of 7,170brt), while three merchantmen—the *Ryujo Maru* (8,370brt), *Horai Maru* (9,192brt) and *Tatsuno Maru* (6,960brt)—and three destroyers were damaged. The *Harukaze* received damage to the bridge, the engine room and the rudder; the *Shikinami's* port propeller was damaged by a near miss, so that her maximum speed was reduced to 24 knots, while the *Shirayuki* was hit by a 15cm shell on the bridge. According to Japanese sources both the *W 2* and the *Sakura Maru* were sunk by torpedoes from their own ships, probably the *Fubuki*.

The Continuation of the Battle of the Java Sea—the Sinking of the Exeter

"May the knowledge be mercifully hidden from them that they died in vain." *(William Ralph Inge (1860-1954), Dean of St Paul's, on the occasion of the action at Zeebrugge)*

At about the same time that the *Perth* and *Houston* left Tandjong Priok, the *Exeter,* escorted by the British destroyer *Encounter* and the American destroyer *Pope,* left Surabaya. The Dutch destroyer *Witte de With* was supposed to sail with them but mechanical troubles kept her in port. The cruiser and two destroyers were ordered to set course for Sunda Strait and then proceed to Colombo. For this purpose they first had to steam parallel to the north coast of Madura at a distance of about 20 miles, thence steer north to pass east of Bawean until the coast of Borneo had been reached, after which they had to alter course to the west. After leaving the minefield protecting the entrance to the naval port of Surabaya they carried out these instructions. At daybreak they were on a westerly course. In the meantime, the landing operations at Kragan were carried out and covered by a Japanese naval force cruising north of Java.

On the morning of March 1st, 1942 this force had reached an area about 100 miles north-west of Bawean, when at 09.30hrs they sighted the three allied ships. For the time being, however, they held back. An enemy report was sent by radio and they waited for reinforcements, which consisted of the heavy cruisers *Ashigara,* flagship of Vice-Admiral Takahashi, and *Myoko,* which steamed at full speed towards the reported position. Less than an hour later the Japanese went into the attack. Four heavy cruisers—*Ashigara, Myoko, Nachi* and *Haguro*—and five destroyers—*Akebono, Ikazuchi, Kawakaze, Yamakaze* and *Inazuma*—as well as aircraft of the fourth and the eleventh airfleet took part in the action.

Until about 11.15hrs the allied ships stayed out of range but then the *Exeter* received a hit in the boiler-room, which caused a fire and resulted in failure of all machinery and guns. The commanding officer decided to scuttle the ship,

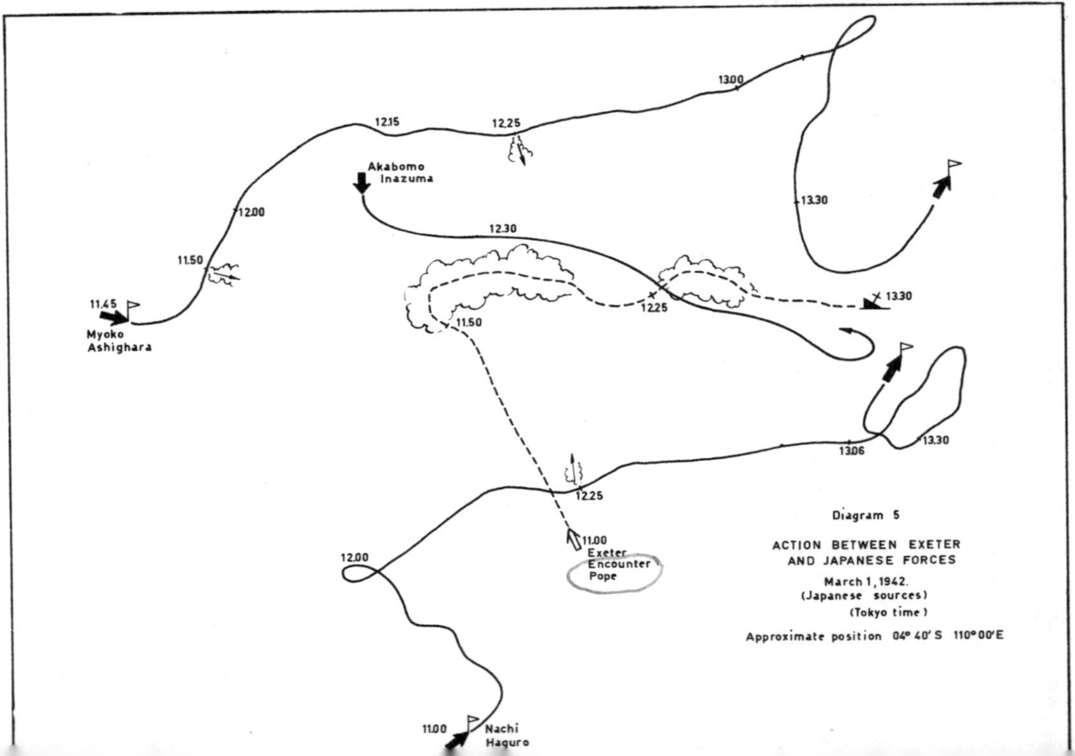

Diagram 5

ACTION BETWEEN EXETER AND JAPANESE FORCES

March 1, 1942.
(Japanese sources)
(Tokyo time)

Approximate position 04° 40′ S 110° 00′E

but the final blow was given by a torpedo launched from the destroyer *Inazuma* (see Table 10 for the times that torpedoes were launched). At about 12.00hrs the *Exeter* went down, soon followed by the *Encounter,* which was hit several times by Japanese gunfire. Finally the *Pope* went under fighting, after she had received a hole beneath the waterline as a result of an attack by six bombers.

The Battle of the Java Sea—Some Minor Engagements

"Correct calculation of risks, by orderly reasoning, is the responsibility of every naval officer who participates in combat, and many who do not." *(E. J. King in* US Navy at War, 1941-1945).

In the western part of the Java Sea the Australian cruiser *Hobart,* the British cruisers *Danae* and *Dragon,* as well as the destroyers *Tenedos* and *Scout,* and the Dutch destroyer *Evertsen* were ordered at midnight on February 27th to carry out a search for a transport fleet, which had been sighted by an aircraft of the RAF on the east coast of Sumatra. However, nothing was found and the ships returned to Tandjong Priok. All ships, except the *Evertsen,* were soon afterwards ordered to sail for Tjilatjap; this was later changed to Trincomalee. Tandjong Priok was frequently bombed by Japanese planes and was no longer a safe harbour. Furthermore there was now a shortage of fuel.

During the sortie to the west, the Dutch destroyer had lost the other ships in a squall and finally returned to Tandjong Priok alone, where it arrived at 14.00hrs on February 28th. Half an hour later the *Evertsen* received orders to leave after dark for Tjilatjap. At 20.30hrs it left harbour and three-quarters of an hour later was clear of the minefield.

The *Evertsen* tried to contact the *Perth* and *Houston* but failed and when it was near the Agenieten Islands the action of Bantam Bay could be seen ahead. It was decided to steam around the area until Pulu Mundu on the Sumatra coast was reached. Here the *Evertsen* went on a southerly course, but at 02.00hrs, just off Dwars in de Weg, an island in Sunda Strait, the destroyer was caught in the searchlights of two ships, which, at a high speed, were also steaming south. They opened fire on the *Evertsen,* which turned away to starboard. In the ensuing gunnery duel the ship received seven hits and the aftership caught fire. As the rear magazine could not be flooded the commanding officer decided to beach the *Evertsen* on the island of Sebuku Besar. The torpedoes were launched; the crew went ashore. The commanding officer of the destroyer had been reluctant to start a night action, as the ship had only been commissioned since December 1st, 1941 and the crew had not had sufficient time for proper training. Furthermore, the fire control had been damaged during the action and she had to fire her guns individually. Also—for unknown reasons—only two of her three boilers were in operation, which meant that the ship could not make maximum speed and was thus hampered in the attempt to escape.

It has always been assumed that it was two cruisers, the *Suzuya* and *Kumano,* which had attacked the *Evertsen* and chased it on to the beach of Sebuku Besar. But a battle report of the 7th Cruiser Division states that two destroyers of the 12th Destroyer Division, the *Murakumo* and *Shirakumo,* both of the Fubuki class, were responsible for this action.

Further to the east another drama was enacted, though this one had a happy end. On Saturday, February 28th, 1942 four American destroyers, the *John D. Edwards, Alden, John D. Ford* and *Paul Jones,* departed from Surabaya at about 17.00hrs. Through the Oostervaarwater they set course for Bali Strait where they had an engagement with three Japanese destroyers, which opened fire on the Americans after the recognition signals had not been answered. The gunnery duel lasted only ten minutes and took place at about 02.30hrs on March 1st. This short action was observed from the shore. The army commander at Banjuwangi reported a naval engagement in a southerly direction, which lasted from 02.28 to 02.35hrs. During the fight the Japanese fire was so accurate that the commanding officer of the *John D. Ford* reported: "The Japanese were undoubtedly using radar, as the opening and subsequent salvos were very close". The *Paul Jones* fired 60 shells per gun in this short action!

However, the American ships managed to break through and on March 4th, 1942 they reached Fremantle safely.

CHAPTER THREE

Some Thoughts on the Battle

The Use of Aircraft and Submarines on February 27th, 1942

"Thus ended the gallant campaign of the Java Sea, conducted against overwhelming odds by officers and men who did the best they could with what they had." *(E. J. King in* US Navy at War, 1941-1945)

It will be apparent from the above narrative that the use of aircraft in the Battle of the Java Sea was a rather one-sided affair. Only the Japanese had used their aircraft to the full, while on the allied side it was a matter of a few exceptions. At the very beginning three A-24 dive-bombers, from 91 Squadron of the 27th Bomber Group, accompanied by ten P-40 fighter aircraft carried out a bombardment on the troopships. The bombers were stationed at Malang, the fighters at Blimbing. At 16.45hrs the Japanese ships were attacked with one bomb of 300 kilograms and two of 250 kilograms. The whole attack lasted only two minutes; the results were nil, though the transport fleet did get an order at 17.04hrs to retreat to the west, but as soon as 17.30hrs course was again altered to the south. Later, when it became clear that the planned landings could not be carried out that night, the ships reversed their course. As already stated above Admiral Helfrich was not informed of this plan of ABDA-air to bombard the invasion fleet.

According to Japanese sources the Japanese navy had two aircraft tenders near Bawean, which supplied the aircraft for the close support of the convoy. These could have been two of the following three ships: *Mizuho, Sanjo Maru* and *Sanuki Maru*. It was customary for Japanese reconnaissance planes to release their bombs before returning to base and the attack on the Combined Striking Force at 17.30hrs should be viewed in this light.

Why was Doorman's force not attacked sooner on February 27th? For his ships had been attacked before, on February 4th at Kangean and on February 15th north of Banka. And now the Japanese again had a fleet without any defence as a target. Practically every day Surabaya had been bombed by aircraft, which had taken off from Kendari. If the bombers had discovered the allied ships while they were passing through the swept channel the ships would have been helpless without sufficient defence and the situation would probably have taken an entirely different turn. On February 27th, however, no bombing of Surabaya took place, though the air raid alarm had sounded three times. What had happened? One of the possible reasons for this, was the attack by about 27 aircraft on the USS *Langley* south of Tjilatjap. These aircraft came from Kendari and as a result of this there would not have been enough aircraft to bomb Surabaya as well.

The loss of the *Langley* around noon was indeed a heavy blow for the allies, because 32 P-40 fighters went down with the ship. These aircraft could have caused some losses to the attacker though the ultimate end of the struggle would not have been different.

Another reason why the Japanese did not carry out an attack on the Combined Striking Force could have been a lack of co-operation between the advancing landing forces and the air actions. It is also possible that no air attacks were allowed on and around February 27th because of the impending landings; the chance of attacking friendly ships and troops was thus eliminated.

As for the use of the shipborne aircraft by the allied ships the following can be said: the *De Ruyter, Java, Exeter* and *Perth* could each carry two aircraft. Of these ships only the *Java* had no catapult. The *Houston* could even carry three aircraft, launched from two catapults. The destroyers *Witte de With* and *Kortenaer* could carry a single aircraft on board, though it is clear that they did not do so, as this impeded the use of guns X and Y. Furthermore, like the

Java, they did not have a catapult, so that the aircraft had to be put overboard by means of a crane. With a view to the forthcoming actions it is plain that the *Java* and both destroyers did not take their aircraft with them. The *Exeter* had a Walrus aircraft on board, but it was unserviceable because of the damage sustained from the near misses of the Japanese bombers.

As for the remaining three ships, the *De Ruyter, Perth* and *Houston*, there was, in the first place the consideration that aircraft fuel had to be carried and probably in the most vulnerable places. Because of the danger of fire it was probably felt inadvisable to carry the aircraft into action especially as a gunnery fight was expected. A second consideration was that a night-action was counted upon, in which case little assistance could be given by the ships' aircraft. Finally, the area in which the forthcoming engagement was expected to take place lay within reach of aircraft based on Surabaya.

Whatever the reasons it was a most regrettable decision. Great delays could arise between the reconnaissance of Japanese naval forces, the transmitting of the sighting report by the aircraft and the reception of this message aboard the flagship.

In the Battle of the Java Sea neither allied nor Japanese submarines played a role. Admiral Helfrich, however, tried, as related before, to concentrate submarines in the most threatened areas of the Java Sea. In or around the area of action were present the British submarine *Truant* (which, however, was not under the direct command of Helfrich), the Dutch submarines *O 19* and *K VIII*, and the American submarines *S 37* and *S 38*. Of these only the *O 19* had witnessed anything of the fighting, but was unable to take up a position to attack. Furthermore, Admiral Doorman, not having command over these submarines could not direct them. Because the Combined Striking Force had few opportunities to form a well trained unit the possibility for such an action was already negligible. Finally it should be noted that since December 1941 the American submarines were used mostly for reconnaissance duties, because they could only be employed in a very limited way, due to a shortage of torpedoes, which were furthermore of inferior quality.

The Japanese submarines have not taken part in the attack, because during this period only a few were operating in the Indonesian waters and of course it was also better they did not operate in the vicinity of the landing fleet to avoid the risk of being sunk by the escort ships.

As for the minelaying operations in the battle area the activities of the *Gouden Leeuw* must be mentioned. This action was limited to the laying of a defensive minefield near the expected landing-places. In the first place this meant that a minefield was laid off the north coast of Madura up to the 20-metre depth-contour but this field need not be considered in this context. On the night of February 26th/27th a second field was laid in the Bay of Tuban, also within the 20-metre depth-contour. By telegram the Naval Commander Surabaya informed the Commander-in-Chief Netherlands Naval Forces as well as the submarines *O 19* and *K VIII*. According to this signal the mines were laid between 06°47'50"S, 112°04'50"E and 06°51'10"S, 112°18'00"E. Admiral Doorman learned of this forthcoming action during the conference on February 26th and was thus fully informed. After the *Gouden Leeuw* completed her minelaying operations, the Naval Commander Surabaya established a danger zone and this was also signalled to the Combined Striking Force commander. It was just on the border of this danger zone that the *Jupiter* blew up at 21.25hrs on February 27th. The destroyer was then in approximately 15 metres of water. Though it is perhaps wrong to jump to the conclusion that the British ship indeed struck a mine, the chances are that this *was* the case. This minefield, as later reports proved, was not laid with the necessary accuracy and it could thus well be possible that the mines were not laid exactly as indicated in the above mentioned message. It is also known that only part of the mines were activated before being put overboard. It is difficult to penetrate the mind of a commanding officer of a ship, who has not carried out his task as is expected of him and if one is inclined to criticise him it is well to remember the words of Shakespeare from *Measure for Measure* (Act II, Scene 2):

"How would you be,
If He, which is the top of judgement, should
But judge you as you are?"

The End

"I am finished. Keep up your hearts!" *(The last words of Admiral Maerten Harpertszoon Tromp when he died in the Battle of Scheveningen August 10th, 1653)*

With the sinking of the *Exeter, Pope* and *Encounter,* allied seapower in the Indies had come to an end. In vain they had tried to keep the Japanese invasion armies from the Java shores. Strictly speaking the matter had been decided at 17.08hrs on February 27th, 1942 when the British cruiser *Exeter* received a hit and had to withdraw from the battle. For it was this which had caused great confusion among the allied ships and through which the attempt by Doorman to reach the Japanese transport fleet had to be abandoned. The only thing that the allies had achieved was the postponement of landings for 24 hours until daylight of March 1st, 1942. They landed at the four designated places: near Merak, in the Bay of Bantam, at Eretan Wetan and at Kragan. It was a hopeless fight as the allied armies lacked the necessary aircraft for support.

On March 2nd Admiral Helfrich left the Netherlands Indies for Colombo by order of the governor-general. As has been stated in Chapter 1 the latter was, on account of his function, Commander-in-Chief of the Netherlands Forces in the East Indies. On March 3rd he received orders from the Netherlands government in London to hand over this command to the new Commander-in-Chief of the Royal Netherlands Navy and to the Commander-in-Chief of the Army. This transfer of command took place on March 4th. The situation in the meantime grew rapidly worse. On March 5th General Ter Poorten came to the conclusion that the possibility of an early capitulation had to be seriously considered.

The governor-general expressed his explicit wish that no fighting should take place in or near Bandung on account of the great number of refugees who were accommodated there. On March 7th the Japanese Commander-in-Chief sent word to the Netherlands Commander-in-Chief that he desired talks with him and the governor-general on the next day. This demand was accompanied by a threat that Bandung would be bombarded if the invitation was refused; thus on March 8th at 13.00hrs a conference started at Kalidjati, during which the Netherlands Indies government decided on an unconditional surrender. Hostilities should end before noon on March 9th. The fight was over. In three months the Japanese had conquered the Netherlands East Indies for which they themselves had reckoned on six months.

To prevent the evacuation of personnel and ships from Java the Japanese had sent a strong naval force into the Indian Ocean, which cruised in the waters south of Java. This force had left Kendari on February 25th and caused considerable loss amongst allied shipping. Seventeen ships were sunk, amongst them the American destroyers *Pillsbury* and *Edsall*, the gunboat *Asheville* and the tanker *Pecos*, the British destroyer *Stronghold* and the Australian sloop *Yarra*. On March 5th aircraft from this Task Force attacked Tjilatjap; 17 ships were sunk and the harbour was completely destroyed. After shelling Christmas Island two days later the force sailed back to Kendari on March 9th.

Some Factors which Contributed to the Defeat

"This is fate." *(Admiral Yamanashi)*

What were the causes of the defeat in this last naval battle for the possession of the Netherlands East Indies? It must be clear to all that the reconnaissance messages during this period were totally insufficient. However, the possibility of success—even if it was very small—was there. Some of the factors, however, which turned the balance in favour of the Japanese were:

(i) Co-operation and co-ordination at the highest level of command was lacking. This was shown most clearly when Rear-Admiral K. W. F. M. Doorman asked for air support, which he did not receive, though this was available—in a small measure—and could and should have been given.

(ii) The Japanese had an air superiority, while on the allied side there was definitely an insufficient number of aircraft available. The Netherlands and American naval flying boats had suffered great losses, and the number that remained was very limited. The air forces of the army too had suffered great losses. Heavy air attacks could not be carried out, while there was a chronic shortage of fighters. The result of this shortage was that at sea the Striking Force was continuously threatened and subjected to air attacks, about which nothing could be done. The fighters that were available were in the first instance needed for the defence of important bases and airfields. Furthermore the anti-aircraft guns of the ships were of little use against the Japanese bombers, which usually flew at heights of about 12,000 feet. The demoralising effect of this was reported several times by the commander of the Combined Striking Force to Admiral Helfrich. The number of fighters at the time of the Battle of the Java Sea must have been about 30, most of which were really in need of maintenance. Fighter aircraft were on their way to Java, such as the 32 P-40 planes aboard the *Langley,* which were practically ready to take part in the battle forthwith. As mentioned previously this ship was sunk on February 27th south of Tjilatjap. Another American ship, the *Seawitch,* entered this port on February 23rd with 27 P-40 aircraft, but these were crated and would therefore need to be assembled before they could be used in battle.

The conquest of Bali and Kupang affected the transport of the necessary aircraft from Australia to Java. After the 20th it was impossible to send fighters via that route as their radius of action was too small.

(iii) The opportunity for combined exercises had been lacking. A weak point of the Combined Striking Force was that she was not formed until the beginning of February 1942, nearly two months after the beginning of the war. Surabaya had then already been bombed and as the force had to go into action immediately, there was no time for the necessary talks and exercises. Furthermore, a safe area in which to carry out exercises was no longer available. Lastly, it should be clear from the previous account that the Striking Force changed its formation several times.

(iv) No joint doctrine existed. As for communications and fire control the differences between the allied fleets were too great. There had been no opportunity to come to one doctrine through conferences on these points which are so essential to naval warfare.

(v) Means of communication were defective. According to Admiral Helfrich there was a joint signalbook in use on the allied fleet, namely:

(a) The Anglo-French code, especially made to code messages quickly and to pass them on by light signals without coding again. It was a lettercode in which various tactical signals were included. It also contained a special section for the transmission of enemy reports.

(b) The air force code, which was used by aircraft. The air force code was made up of the Self-Evident code and was supplied to all allied ships. It was laid down that this Self-Evident code should be used by all allies for transmitting reconnaissance signals.

Other reliable sources state, however, that there were no joint signalbooks on board the ships. Neither was there an allied system for signalling with flags. This shortcoming was partly solved by attaching British and American signalmen on board the flagship. Also the ultra high frequency (UHF) R/T installation did not stand up to the heavy vibrations caused by gunfire. As on board the *De Ruyter* the searchlights, which could also be used for signalling purposes, were destroyed by the air pressure of her own guns, the handsignal lamp was really the only means to communicate!

(vi) The crews of the ships were overtired. Already a great demand had been made on the pilots, observers and other members of the crews of the aircraft—both naval and army. They had reached the limit of their power of endurance and morale. Around February 18th General Brereton had received information from the medical staff of bomber command about the bad physical and morale resistance of the flying personnel.

(vii) The allies were entirely ignorant of the Japanese long-range torpedoes and thus the element of technical surprise played an important role.

(viii) It was remarkable how well the Japanese were in touch with the movements of the Combined Striking Force. From 11.10hrs all course and speed alterations of this force were passed on by Japanese reconnaissance planes to their own ships. It was thus impossible for the allies to make use of the element of surprise.

Lastly something should be said about the high figure of casualties on the allied side, especially on board the cruisers *De Ruyter* and *Java,* where the percentages of killed were respectively 79 per cent and 96 per cent. The *Houston* counted 65 per cent killed, the *Electra* 62 per cent, the *Perth* 55 per cent and the *Kortenaer* about 37 per cent. Some factors which could have contributed to this large figure of men killed in combat are:

(i) When the *Java* went under a great number of explosions took place.

(ii) Aboard the *De Ruyter* the explosion of the 40mm ammunition caused many casualties.

(iii) Not until the *De Ruyter* was stopped, did the crew abandon ship and many died in the burning oil, which was pouring freely from the ships.

(iv) The crews were morally and physically exhausted, so that many probably lacked the strength to fight for their lives.

(v) On February 28th at 06.19hrs the hospital ship *Op ten Noort* had been directed to the place of destruction of the *De Ruyter, Java, Encounter* and *Kortenaer,* but at 14.40hrs the ship was intercepted about 40 miles south of Bawean, by two Japanese destroyers, which were, according to a Japanese report, the *Amatsukaze* and the *Murasame.* The *Op ten Noort* was directed to a place on the north coast of the island to be searched. The R/T was put out of action and it was only after two days that the ship was allowed to proceed to Bandjermasin.

(vi) During the last conference on February 26th Rear-Admiral Doorman had given verbal instructions to the commanding officers of his ships that if a ship was put out of action it "must be left to the mercy of the enemy". That the *Encounter* was ordered to pick up the survivors of the *Kortenaer* can be understood because the British destroyer had practically no fuel left so she had to refuel anyway and furthermore she could hardly keep up with the four cruisers.

One final remark must be made here. One of the reasons for the rapid advance of the Japanese forces in the Indian archipelago was the presence of the many airfields. Before the war there had been a sharp controversy between the army and the navy. The army advocated a great number of airfields, which, strewn amongst the many islands, could serve as bases for landbased aircraft, which could destroy a potential opponent with hostile intentions. The navy on the other hand opposed this plan because they foresaw that the enemy air force would in the first instance attack these airfields, destroy the aircraft based there and then capture and use them for their own purposes. Therefore, the navy believed in a plan to use seaplanes to carry out bombardments and reconnaissance. An additional advantage would be the ease with which bases could be kept secret from the enemy. What was needed were depot ships for the necessary maintenance of the aircraft, and these would in any case be cheaper than an airfield with the buildings appertaining to it and furthermore they would be far more difficult targets for the opposing bombers.

The course of events in the Netherlands East Indies has proved that the army point of view was fatal, especially as the airfields which were in use were weakly defended and insufficient precautionary measures were taken to destroy the fields so as to deny the use of them to the enemy.

PART II
STATISTICAL DATA

APPENDIX ONE

Details of the Japanese Army Intended for the Invasion of the Netherlands East Indies

The Japanese invasion army, intended for the capture of the Netherlands East Indies, was the 16th Army under the command of Lieutenant-General Imamura.
The composition of this army was as follows:

General Staff
Chief of Staff: Major-General Okasaki.

2nd Division
Commanding Officer: Major-General Muruyama.
This division was intended for the invasion of West Java (landings near Merak and in Bantam Bay).

38th Division
Commanding Officer: Major-General Sano.
This division had already taken part in the capture of Hong Kong and was composed of:

(a) The 228th Regiment Infantry, concentrated at Davao, and intended for the invasion of Ambon and Timor.
(b) The 229th Regiment Infantry, concentrated at Camranh Bay, and intended for the invasion of West and Palembang.
(c) The 230th Regiment Infantry, also stationed at Camrahn Bay, and intended for the invasion of West Java together with the 2nd Division.

48th Division
Commanding Officer: Major-General Tsuchihashi.
This division had first taken part in the actions against the Philippines before being used against the Netherlands Indies. It was concentrated at Davao and intended for the invasion of Bali and East Java.

Sakaguchi Brigade (56th Regimental Group)
Commanding Officer: Colonel Sakaguchi.
Concentrated at Davao, this brigade was intended for the invasion of Tarakan, Balikpapan and Bandjermasin and ultimately East Java. It was composed of the 146th Regiment Infantry and units of armoured vehicles, field artillery, military engineers and medical service.
The following naval units were attached to the 16th Army:

Kure 1st Special Naval Landing Force
Concentrated at Davao and intended for the capture of Ambon. The force consisted of three rifle companies and one machine gun company. Total strength 820 men.

Kure 2nd Special Naval Landing Force
Also concentrated at Davao and intended for the capture of Tarakan, Balikpapan and Bandjermasin. This force consisted of three companies, one machine gun company and one anti-aircraft battery. Total strength 1,000 men.

Sasebo Combined Special Naval Landing Force
Concentrated at Davao and intended for the capture of Menado, Kendari and Makassar. The force consisted of the 1st and 2nd Unit, each of 800 men. Each unit was composed of three rifle companies and one machine gun company.

Yokosuka 1st Special Naval Landing Force
This was a parachute unit, concentrated at Davao and intended for the capture of Menado. The force consisted of three companies, with a total of 519 paratroops.

Yokosuka 3rd Special Naval Landing Force
Concentrated at Davao and intended for the capture of Timor. This force was also a paratroop unit and consisted of three rifle companies, with a total strength of about 1,000 men.

APPENDIX TWO

Details of the Southern Force of the Japanese Navy

The naval forces, which had to escort the units of the 16th Army to the various points of attack in the Netherlands East Indies, were called the *Southern Force.* It was divided into three forces and came under the command of Vice-Admiral Kondo, Commander-in-Chief of the 2nd Japanese Fleet. Directly under his command were:

3rd Battle Squadron (2nd Division): *Kongo* (flag), *Haruna.*
4th Cruiser Squadron (Viced-Admiral Ozawa): *Atago* (flag), *Takao, Maya.*
4th Destroyer Division: *Arashi, Hagikaze, Nowaki, Maikaze.*
6th Destroyer Division: *Hibiki, Akatsuki.*
The 1st Air Fleet was also under the overall command of Vice-Admiral Kondo. This Fleet, under command of Vice-Admiral Nagumi, consisted of:
1st Carrier Squadron: *Akagi, Kaga.*
2nd Carrier Squadron: *Soryu, Hiryu.*
3rd Battle Squadron (1st Division): *Hiei, Kirishima.*
8th Cruiser Squadron (1st Division): *Tone, Chikuma.*

Eastern Force
The Eastern Force came under the command of Vice-Admiral Takahashi and was intended for the landings at Menado, Kendari, Ambon, Makassar, Timor and Bali.

MENADO

Convoy: eight transports carrying the Sasebo Combined Special Naval Landing Force.

28 Transport-aircraft carrying the Yokosuka 1st Special Naval Landing Force.

Convoy escort: under the command of Rear-Admiral Tanaka.

Cruiser: *Jintsu* (flag).

2nd Destroyer Flotilla:

8th Destroyer Division (1st Group): *Oshio, Asashio.*

15th Destroyer Division: *Natsushio, Kuroshio, Oyashio, Hayashio.*

16th Destroyer Division: *Yukikaze, Tokitsukaze, Hatsukaze, Amatsukaze.*

Air Group under command of Rear-Admiral Fujita.

11th Seaplane Tender Division: *Chitose, Mizuho.*

Patrol boats: *P 39.*

Base Force under command of Rear-Admiral Kubo.

1st Base Force:

Cruiser: *Nagara* (flag).

Patrol boats: *P 1, P 2, P 34.*

21st Minesweeper Division: *W 7, W 8, W 9, W 11, W 12.*

1st Submarine-chaser Division: *Ch 1, Ch 2, Ch 3.*

Covering Force under command of Rear-Admiral Takagi.

5th Cruiser Squadron: *Nachi* (flag), *Haguro, Myoko.* (The *Myoko* was damaged during a bombasrdment of Davao on January 4th and had to return to Sasebo for repairs. She left this port on February 20th and arrived at Makassar six days later.

6th Destroyer Division (2nd Group): *Ikazuchi, Inazuma.*

KENDARI

Convoy: six transports carrying the Sasebo Combined Special Naval Landing Force.

Convoy escort under command of Rear-Admiral Kubo.

Cruiser: *Nagara* (flag).

15th Destroyer Division: as for Menado.

16th Destroyer Division: as for Menado.

1st Base Force:

21st Minesweeper Division: *W 7, W 8, W 9, W 11, W 12.*

1st Submarine-chaser Division: *Ch 1, Ch 2.*
Air Group under command of Rear-Admiral Fujita.
2nd Carrier Squadron: *Hiryu, Soryu.* (These carriers did not operate under the direct control of Rear-Admiral Fujita. They had to provide protection for the eastern flank by bombing Ambon during the landings at Kendari. The ships arrived in the waters east of Halmahera on January 23rd).
11th Seaplane Tender Division: *Chitose, Mizuho.*
Patrol boats: *P 34, P 39.*
Covering Force under command of Rear-Admiral Takagi.
As for Menado.

AMBON
Convoy: ten transports carrying the Kure 1st Special Naval Landing Force and the 228th Regiment Infantry.
Convoy escort under command of Rear-Admiral Tanaka.
Cruiser: *Jintsu* (flag).
2nd Destroyer Flotilla:
8th Destroyer Division: *Asashio, Oshio, Michishio, Arashio.*
15th Destroyer Division: *Natsushio, Kuroshio, Oyashio, Hayashio.*
16th Destroyer Division: *Amatsukaze, Hatsukaze, Yukikaze, Tokitsukaze.*
21st Minesweeper Division: *W 7, W 8, W 9, W 11, W 12.* (The *W 9* was sunk by a mine in the Bay of Ambon on February 2nd, while on this same occasion the *W 11* and *W 12* were damaged).
1st Submarine-chaser Division: *Ch 1, Ch 2, Ch 3.*
Air Group under command of Rear-Admiral Fujita.
11th Seaplane Tender Division: *Chitose, Mizuho.*
Patrol boats: *P 34, P 39.*
Covering Force under command of Rear-Admiral Takagi.
5th Cruiser Squadron: *Nachi* (flag), *Haguro, Ikazuchi* (destroyer).
7th Destroyer Division: *Ushio, Sazanami.*

MAKASSAR
Convoy: six transports carrying the Sasebo Combined Special Naval Landing Force.
Convoy escort (1st Base Force) under command of Rear-Admiral Kubo.

Cruiser: *Nagara* (flag).
8th Destroyer Division: *Asashio, Oshio, Michishio, Arashio.*
15th Destroyer Division: *Natsushio, Kuroshio, Oyashio, Hayashio.* (The *Natsushio* was sunk by the *S 37* on February 9th, 1942, in position 05° 36' S, 119° 24' E).
21st Destroyer Division: *Wakaba, Nenohi, Natsushimo.*
21st Minesweeper Division: *W 7, W 8.*
2nd Submarine-chaser Division: *Ch 13, Ch 14, Ch 15.*
1st Submarine-chaser Division: *Ch ?, P ?, P ?.*
Minelayers: *Tsukushi, Aotaka.*
Air Group under command of Rear-Admiral Fujita.
11th Seaplane Tender Division: *Chitose, Mizuho, Sanuki Maru.*
Patrol boat: *P ?.*
Support Force (was stationed in the Balikpapan area).
24th Destroyer Division: *Kawakaze, Umikaze.*
9th Destroyer Division: *Asagumo, Natsugumo, Minegumo.*
30th Minesweeper Division: *W 17, W 18.*
11th Minesweeper Division: *W 15, W 16.*
Covering Force under command of Rear-Admiral Takagi.
5th Cruiser Squadron: *Nachi* (flag), *Haguro.*
Destroyers: *Akebono, Ikazuchi.*

TIMOR
Convoy: nine transports carrying the 228th Infantry Regiment.
? transport aircraft carrying the Yokosuka 3rd Special Naval Landing Force.
Convoy escort under command of Rear-Admiral Tanaka.
Cruiser: *Jintsu* (flag).
2nd Destroyer Flotilla:
7th Destroyer Division: *Ushio, Sazanami.*
15th Destroyer Division: *Natsushio, Kuroshio, Oyashio, Hayashio.*
16th Destroyer Division: *Hatsukaze, Yukikaze, Amatsukaze, Tokitsukaze.*
21st Minesweeper Division: *W ?, W ?, W ?.*
Air Group:
Seaplane tender: *Mizuho.*
Patrol boat: *P ?.*

Covering Force under command of Rear-Admiral Takagi.
5th Cruiser Squadron: *Nachi,* Haguro.
Destroyers: *Akebono, Inazuma, Yamakaze, Kawakaze.*

BALI
Convoy: two transports, *Sagami Maru* (7,189brt) and *Sasako Maru* (9,258brt), carrying an infantry battalion (the Kanemura Detachment) of the 48th Division.
Convoy escort:
8th Destroyer Division: *Oshio, Asashio, Michishio, Arashio.*
Covering Force under command of Rear-Admiral Kubo.
Cruiser: *Nagara* (flag).
21st Destroyer Division: *Wakaba, Hatsushimo, Nenohi.*

Central Force
The Central Force came under the command of Vice-Admiral Takahashi and was intended for the landings at Tarakan, Balikpapan and Bandjermasin.

TARAKAN
Convoy: 16 transports carrying the Sakaguchi Brigade and the Kure 2nd Special Naval Landing Force from Davao.
Convoy escort under command of Rear-Admiral Nishimura.
Cruiser: *Naka* (flag).
4th Destroyer Flotilla:
2nd Destroyer Division: *Harusame, Samidare, Yudachi, Murasame.*
9th Destroyer Division: *Asagumo, Minegumo, Natsugumo.*
24th Destroyer Division: *Umikaze, Kawakaze, Yamakaze, Suzukaze.*
Air Group:
Seaplane tenders: *Sanyo Maru, Sanuki Maru.*
Oiler: one oiler.
Base Force under command of Rear-Admiral Hirose.
2nd Base Force:
Patrol boats: *P 36, P 37, P 38.*
11th Minesweeper Division: *W 13, W 14, W 15, W 16.* (The *W 13* and *W 14* were sunk at Tarakan on January 12th by a coastal battery).
30th Minesweeper Division: *W 17, W 18.*

31st Submarine-chaser Divison: *Ch 10, Ch 11, Ch 12.*
The necessary auxiliaries.

BALIKPAPAN
Convoy: 16 transports carrying the Sakaguchi Brigade and the Kure 2nd Special Naval Landing Force from Tarakan.
Convoy escort: under the command of Rear-Admiral Nishimura.
As for Tarakan, without the *Yamakaze* and *Suzukaze.*
Air Group:
As for Tarakan.
Base Force under command of Rear-Admiral Hirose.
As for Tarakan without the *W 13, W 14, Ch 10* and *Ch 11.*

BANDJERMASIN
Overland: One battalion minus one company of the Sakaguchi Brigade under command of Colonel Yamamoto.
Amphibian: One company of the overland battalion of the Sakaguchi Brigade under command of Captain Yoshibumi Okamoto.

Western Force
The Western Force came under the command of Vice-Admiral Ozawa aboard the *Chokai* and was intended for the landings at Banka and Palembang and consisted of an Advance Force and a Main Force.

ADVANCE FORCE
Convoy: eight transports carrying part of the 229th Infantry Regiment.
Convoy escort under command of Rear-Admiral Hashimoto.
Cruiser: *Sendai* (flag).
20th Destroyer Division: *Asagiri.*
11th Destroyer Division: *Fubuki, Hatsuyuki, Shirayuki.*
1st Minesweeper Division: *W 1, W 2, W 3, W 4, W 5.*
11th Submarine-chaser Division: *Ch 7, Ch 8.*

MAIN FORCE
Under command of Vice-Admiral Ozawa aboard the *Chokai.*

Convoy: 14 transports carrying the 229th Infantry Regiment (minus the part of the Advance Force) and a battalion of the 230th Infantry Regiment.
Convoy escort:
Training ship: *Kashii.*
20th Destroyer Division: *Yugiri, Amagiri.*
Escort vessel: *Shimushu.*
11th Submarine-chaser Division: *Ch 9.*
Base Force.
Minelayer: *Hatsutaka.*
Minesweepers: *W ?, W ?.*
Transportship: *Konyu Maru.*
Tanker: *Eikyo Maru.*
Covering Force under command of Vice-Admiral Ozawa.
4th Cruiser Division: *Chokai* (flag).
Cruiser: *Yura.*
7th Cruiser Division: *Mikuma, Mogami, Suzuya, Kumano.*
12th Destroyer Division: *Shirakumo.*
19th Destroyer Division: *Ayanami, Isonami.*
Air Group under command of Rear-Admiral Sumida.
4th Carrier Squadron: *Ryujo* with the 3rd Air Group.
19th Destroyer Division: *Shikinami.*

Java Force
For the direct attack and the occupation of Java a combined Java Force was formed, consisting of a force for Western Java and one for Eastern Java under command of Vice-Admiral Takahashi aboard the *Ashigara,* accompanied by the cruiser *Myoko* and two destroyers, the *Ikazuchi* and *Akebono.*

FORCE FOR WESTERN JAVA
Left Camranh Bay on February 18th for landings at Merak, Bantam Bay and Eretan Wetan.
Convoy: 56 transports carrying the Headquarters of the 16th Army, the 2nd Division and the 230th Infantry Regiment.
Convoy escort under command of Rear-Admiral Hara.
Cruisers: *Natori, Yura.*
5th Destroyer Division: *Asakaze, Harukaze, Hatakaze.*

11th Destroyer Division: *Fubuki, Shirayuki, Hatsuyuki.*
12th Destroyer Division: *Murakumo, Shirakumo.*
6th Destroyer Division: *Hibiki, Akatsuki.*
22nd Destroyer Division: *Satsuki, Fumitsuki, Nagatsuki, Minazuki.*
21st Torpedoboat Division: *Hatsukari, Chidori.*
Air Group under command of Rear-Admiral Kakuta.
Aircraft carrier: *Ryujo.*
Destroyer: *Shikinami.*
Base Force under command of Rear-Admiral Hirose.
2nd Base Force:
Minelayer: *Shirataka.*
1st Minesweeper Division: *W 1, W 2, W 3, W 4, W 5.*
Covering Force under command of Rear-Admiral Kurita.
7th Cruiser Division: *Mikuma* (flag), *Mogami, Suzuya, Kumano.*
Destroyers: *Akebono, Ikazuchi.*

FORCE FOR EASTERN JAVA
Left Jolo on February 19th for landings near Kragan.
Convoy: 41 transports carrying the 48th Division and the Sakaguchi Brigade.
Convoy escort under command of Rear-Admiral Nishimura.
4th Destroyer Squadron under command of Rear-Admiral Nishimura.
Cruiser: *Naka* (flag).
9th Destroyer Division: *Asagumo, Minegumo, Natsugumo.* (The *Natsugumo* stayed with the transport fleet during the Battle of the Java Sea).
2nd Destroyer Division: *Murasame, Yudachi, Harusame, Samidare.*
2nd Destroyer Squadron under command of Rear-Admiral Tanaka.
Cruiser: *Jintsu* (flag).
16th Destroyer Division: *Yukikaze, Tokitsukaze, Amatsukaze, Hatsukaze.*
24th Destroyer Division: *Umikaze, Yamakaze, Kawakaze.* (The *Umikaze* stayed with the transport fleet during the Battle of the Java Sea).
Covering Force under command of Rear-Admiral Takagi.

(Takagi was in tactical command of the Japanese during the Battle of the Java Sea on February 27th, 1942).
5th Cruiser Division: *Nachi* (flag), *Haguro.*
7th Destroyer Division: *Ushio, Sazanami.* (The 7th Destroyer Division came also under the command of the 2nd Destroyer Squadron during the Battle of the Java Sea).
11th Minesweeper Division: *W 15, W 16.*
30th Minesweeper Division: *W 17, W 18.*
21st Submarine-chaser Division: *Ch 4, Ch 5, Ch 6, Ch 16, Ch 17, Ch 18.*
Minelayer: *Wakataka.*
Air Group.
Seaplane tenders: *Mizuho, Sanjo Maru, Sanuki Maru.*

Task Force which operated in the Indian Ocean (February 25th-March 9th, 1942)
This task force consisted of two forces:

Carrier Striking Force, under command of Vice-Admiral Nagumo.
1st Carrier Division: *Akagi, Kaga.*
2nd Carrier Division: *Soryu, Hiryu.*
3rd Cruiser Division: *Hiriki, Kirishima.*
8th Cruiser Division: *Tone, Chikuma.*
1at Destroyer Squadron: *Abukuma.*
17th Destroyer Squadron: *Tanikaze, Isokaze, Hamakaze, Urakaze.*
18th Destroyer Squadron: *Shiranuhi, Kasumi.*
27th Destroyer Squadron: *Ariake, Yugure.*
Six supply ships.

Main Force of the Southern Force, under command of Vice-Admiral Kondo.
3rd Battleship Division: *Kongo, Haruna.*
4th Cruiser Division: *Atago, Takao.*
4th Destroyer Division: *Arashi, Nowaki.*
15th Destroyer Division: *Hayashio.*

APPENDIX THREE

Details of the Japanese Air Force Intended for the Invasion of the Netherlands East Indies

The Japanese air force was not a separate service like the navy and army, but consisted of two entirely independent forces, which supported both the navy and army in their actions.

The Naval Air Force gave support to surface ships and was also responsible for coastal defence, anti-submarine patrols and convoy protection. It consisted to two air fleets: the 11th and 1st Air Fleet. The 11th Air Fleet, commanded by Vice-Admiral N. Tsukahashi, was shore-based and assisted in the invasion of Indo-China, Malaya and the Netherlands East Indies. This fleet consisted of three Air Flotillas, the 21st, the 22nd and the 23rd. The former and the latter consisted of three groups, the 22nd of two groups. The 11th Air Fleet had to co-operate with the Southern Fleet under Vice-Admiral Kondo. The total strength was 245 shore-based aircraft (94 fighters, 12 reconnaissance aircraft and 139 bombers).

The 21st and 23rd Air Flotillas were based at Davao from December 23rd, 1941 and at Jolo from December 26th respectively and were intended for actions against the Netherlands Indies. Their operational area was divided by the 122nd degree of longitude. The 21st Air Flotilla (1 Air Attack Force) was allotted to the eastern part and carried out its first bombardment on Menado on December 24th, 1941. After the fall of Kendari on January 24th, 1942 it was based there.

The 23rd Air Flotilla (2 Air Attack Force) was allotted to the western part and had to operate against Tarakan, Balikpapan and Bandjermasin. The small aircraft-carrier *Ryujo* and four seaplane tenders were also incorporated in the 11th Air Fleet. The 1st Air Fleet, under command of Vice-Admiral Nagumo, was also attached to the Southern Fleet.

The Army Air Force consisted of five Air Divisions. The 3rd Air Division, with a total strength of 354 aircraft (146 fighters, 36 reconnaissance aircraft and 172 bombers), supported the 25th Japanese Army in Malaya, but was also designated to co-operate with the Western Force.

APPENDIX FOUR

Details of the Netherlands Forces at Palembang, Western Java and Eastern Java on January 10th, 1942

Palembang

NAVY

Pro Patria (minelayer)

p 37, *P 38*, *P 39*, *P 40* — auxiliary patrol vessels

ARMY

Four infantry companies

One machine gun company

Light guns of 7.5cm

Two 40mm AA guns (on the airfield Palembang I)

ARMY AIR FORCE

Bombers and reconnaissance aircraft:

On January 18th, 1942 the 225 Bomber Group was formed at Palembang and on January 30th came under the command of Air Commodore H. J. F. Hunter. On February 1st, 1942 the 226 Fighter Group was formed under the command of Air Commodore S. F. Vincent; this was made up from the remnants of 224 Fighter Group from Singapore and 266 Group coming from Great Britain. There were plans for an overall command of all British air forces in Sumatra, Air Headquarters, under command of Air

Commodore B. J. Silly. On February 2nd headquarters for the Royal Air Force was established at Palembang, which was moved to Sukabumi on Java exactly two weeks later. It was not until February 7th that the Royal Air Force and the Royal Australian Air Force at Palembang were put under the command of ABDA-air.

Realising the importance of Palembang (oil-refineries and airfields) it is obvious that there were not enough troops for her defence. Actually the forces were just enough to maintain order. On February 5th, 1942 the Xth Infantry Battalion was sent from Western Java to Palembang. On January 30th some anti-aircraft artillery (among others six guns of 3.7cm) had arrived from Singapore. Unfortunately the ammunition was lost when the ship in which it was carried was torpedoed and sunk in the beginning of February 1942. Another ship carrying guns and ammunition of 3.7cm ran aground on its way from Singapore to Palembang and the valuable cargo did not reach its destination until February 11th.

Furthermore, when reinforcements for Singapore could no longer be sent there General Wavell decided that the 1st Australian Division should be transported to Sumatra and the 2nd Australian Division to Java. After January 10th, 1942 British aircraft arrived at Palembang to give protection in Sunda Strait and Banka Strait to the so-called Singapore convoys and to operate against Malaya.

On February 5th a second infantry battalion (the IXth) was sent from Western Java. This one was bound for Banka and Billiton.

Western Java

NAVY

Various ships at Tandjong Priok

ARMY

The 1st Division (Major-General W. Schilling) consisting of two infantry regiments with motorised troops, anti-armour and anti-aircraft guns.

About 3,000 men reserve troops armed with carbine machine-guns, machine-guns and tommyguns.

Two cavalry regiments, one motorised, one horse.
One reconnaissance and security detachment.
One artillery regiment consisting of 12 guns of 10.5cm and 12 guns of 7.5cm.
Futhermore there were four guns of 7.5cm and two guns of 5cm as well as four anti-aircraft guns of 8cm, two anti-aircraft guns of 40mm and four anti-aircraft guns of 20mm.
One company of pioneers.
Australian troops, the so-called Black Force, under the command of Brigadier-General A. S. Blackburn. This force consisted of three motorised battalions totalling about 2,200 men including the staff and medical branch.
Furthermore there was one squadron of 16 light tanks of the King's Own Hussars (B Squadron), as well as two American batteries of the 131 Battalion Field Artillery.

Army Air Force
Bombers and fighters:
At the disposal of the divisional commander were:
9 Hurricane fighters and
4 Curtiss Falcons.
On February 28th there were at
Bantam Bay: 1 infantry section, 1 machine gun section, 1 gun of 7.5cm.
Merak: 1 infantry section, 1 machine gun section, 1 searchlight.

Eastern Java
NAVY
Various ships at Surabaya
Reconnaissance and bomber aircraft.

ARMY
The 3rd Division (Major-General G. A. Ilgen) consisting of three infantry regiments with motorised troops, anti-armour and anti-aircraft guns.
One motorised company.
Three infantry battalions at Madura (Barisan Corps).
Two infantry companies (Legion of Mangkunegoro).
Reserve troops at Kediri and Surabaya.

One detachment of cavalry, motorised.
Three motorised batteries of three guns each.
One American battery of Field Artillery (2nd battery of the 131 Regiment Field Artillery).
One mobile detachment of three batteries of four guns of 7.5cm at Madura.
One battalion Coastal Artillery with the following batteries.
Menari: two batteries of three guns of 15cm, one battery of four guns of 7.5cm, two guns of 20mm anti-aircraft, four searchlights.
Kedong-Tjowek: one battery of five guns of 15cm, one battery of four guns of 7.5cm, two guns of 20mm anti-aircraft, and two searchlights.
Piring (Madura): one battery of four guns of 12cm, one battery of four guns of 7.5cm, two guns of 20mm anti-aircraft, two searchlights.
Tompeng (Madura): one battery of four guns of 15cm, two searchlights.
On the harbour front of Surabaya: one battery of three guns of 7.5cm, one battery of two guns of 7.5cm, one battalion of anti-aircraft artillery, engineers for the operation of the searchlights and one company of pioneers.

ARMY AIR FORCE
Bombers and fighters:
On January 31st, 1942 there were the following aircraft on Java:

17	B-17 and Liberator bombers	*American*
36	Glenn Martin bombers	*Dutch*
31	Buffalo fighters	
8	Curtiss Hawk fighters	
14	Curtiss Interceptor fighters	
34	P-40 fighters	
9	Lockheed-12 reconnaissance aircraft	
18	Curtiss Falcon reconnaissance aircraft	

On March 1st there were available in Java 50 bombers, 53 fighters and eight dive bombers!

APPENDIX FIVE

'ABDACOM' Directive to Supreme Commander, Dated January 3rd, 1942

By agreement among the governments of Australia, Netherlands, United Kingdom and United States, hereinafter referred to as the ABDA Governments.

(1) Area. A strategic area has been constituted to comprise initially all land and sea areas including general regions of Burma, Malaya, Netherlands East Indies and Philippine Islands more precisely defined in Annexure 1. This area will be known as ABDA area.

(2) Forces. You have been designated as Supreme Commander of ABDA area and of all armed forces afloat, ashore and in the air of ABDA Governments which are or will be (a) stationed in area (b) located in Australian territory when such forces have been allotted by respective Governments for service in or in support of the ABDA area. You are not authorised to transfer from territories of an ABDA Government land forces of the Government without consent of local commander or his Government.

(3) The Deputy Supreme Commander and if required a Commander of the Combined Naval Forces and the Commander of Combined Air Forces will be jointly designated by the ABDA Governments.

(4) No Government will materially reduce its armed forces assigned to your area nor any commitment made by it for reinforcing its forces in your area except after

giving to other Governments and to you timely information pertaining thereto.

(5) Strategic concept and policy. The basic strategic concept of the ABDA Governments for conduct of war in your area is not only in the immediate future to maintain as many key positions as possible but to take offensive at the earliest opportunity and ultimately to conduct an all-out offensive against Japan. The first essential is to gain general air superiority at the earliest moment through employment of concentrated air power. The piece-meal employment of air forces should be minimised. Your operations should be conducted as to further preparations for the offensive.

(6) General strategic policy will be therefore:

(a) to hold Malaya barrier defined as line Malay Peninsula, Sumatra, Java, North Australia as basic defensive position of ABDA area and to operate sea, land and air forces in as great depth as possible forward of barrier in order to oppose Japanese southward advance;

(b) to hold Burma and Australia as essential support positions for the area and Burma as essential to support of China and to defence of India;

(c) to re-establish communications through Dutch East Indies with Luzon to support Philippines garrison;

(d) to maintain essential communications within the area.

(7) Duties, responsibilities and authorities of Supreme Commander. You will co-ordinate in ABDA area strategical operations of all armed forces of ABDA Governments where desirable to arrange formation of task forces whether national or inter-national for executing specific operations and appointing any officers irrespective of seniority or nationality to command such task forces.

(8) While you have no responsibilities in respect of the internal administration of the respective forces under

your command you are authorised to direct and co-ordinate the creation and development of administrative facilities and the broad allocation of war materials.

(9) You will dispose of reinforcements which from time to time may be despatched to the area by ABDA Governments.

(10) You are authorised to require from commanders of the armed forces under your command such reports as you deem necessary in discharging your responsibilities as supreme commander.

(11) You are authorised to control the issue of all communiques concerning the forces under your command.

(12) Through channels specified in paragraph 18 you may submit recommendations to the ABDA Governments on any matters pertaining to the furthering of your mission.

(13) Limitations. Your authority and control with respect to the various portions of ABDA area and to forces assigned thereto will normally be exercised through commanders duly appointed by their respective Governments. Interference is to be avoided in administrative processes of armed forces of any of the ABDA Governments including free communication between them and their respective Governments. No alterations or revision is to be made in basic tactical organisations of such forces and each national component of a task force will normally operate under its own commander and will not be sub-divided into small units for attachment to other national components of task forces except in cases of urgent necessity. In general your instructions and orders will be limited to those necessary for effective co-ordination of forces in execution of your mission.

(14) Relations with ABDA Governments. The ABDA Governments will jointly and severally support you in the execution of duties and responsibilities as herein defined and in the exercising of authority herein delegated and limited. Commanders of all sea, land

and air forces within your area will be immediately informed by their respective Governments that from a date to be notified all orders and instructions issued by you in conformity with the provision of this directive will be considered by such commanders as emanating from their respective Governments.

(15) In the unlikely event that any of your immediate subordinates after making due representation to you still considers obedience to your orders would jeopardise national interests of his country to an extent unjustified by the general situation in ABDA area he has the right subject to your being immediately notified of such intention to appeal direct to his own Government before carrying out orders. Such appeals will be made by most expeditious methods and copies of appeals will be communicated simultaneously to you.

(16) Staff and assumption of command. Your staff will include officers of each of ABDA Powers.
You are empowered to communicate immediately with national commanders in area with view to obtaining staff officers essential your earliest possible assumption of command. Your additional staff requirements will be communicated as soon as possible to ABDA Governments through channels of communication described in paragraph 18.

(17) You will report when you are in position effectively carry essential functions of supreme command so your assumption of command may be promulgated to all concerned.

(18) Superior Authority. As supreme commander of ABDA area you will always be responsible to ABDA Governments through agency defined in Annexure II.

ANNEXURE I—BOUNDARIES OF ABDA AREA

The ABDA area is bounded as follows:

North. By boundary between India and Burma, thence eastward along Chinese frontier and coastline to latitude 030 degrees north, thence along parallel 030 degrees north

to meridian 140 degrees east. (NOTE. Indo-China and Thailand are NOT included in this area).
East. By meridian 140 degrees east from 030 degrees to the Equator, thence east to longitude 141 degrees east, thence south to the boundary of Dutch New Guinea (and to) coast on south coast, thence east along southern New Guinea Coast to meridian 143 degrees east, then south down this meridian to the coast of Australia.
South. By the northern coast of Australia from meridian 143 degrees east westward to meridian 114 degrees east, thence north-west ward to latitude 015 degrees south, longitude 092 degrees east.
West. By meridian 092 degrees east.

(2) Forces assigned to ABDA and adjacent are authorised to extend their operations into other areas as may be required.

ANNEXURE II

(1) On all important military matters not within the jurisdiction of supreme commander of ABDA area. US Chiefs of Staff and representatives in Washington of British Chiefs of Staff will constitute agency for developing and submitting recommendations for decisions by President of US, and by British Prime Minister and Minister of Defence. Among Chief matters on which decision will be required are:

(a) Provision of reinforcements.
(b) Major changes in policy.
(c) Departures from supreme commander's directive.

(2) This agency will function as follows:

(a) Any proposals coming either from Supreme Commander or from any of the ABDA Governments will be submitted to Chiefs of Staff Committee both in Washington and in London.
(b) The Chiefs of Staff Committee in London will immediately telegraph to their representatives in Washington to say whether or not they will be telegraphing any opinion.

(c) On receipt of these opinions the USACs of S and representatives in Washington of British Cs of S, will develop and submit their recommendations to President and by telegraphing to Prime Minister and Minister of Defence. Prime Minister will then inform the President whether he is in agreement with these recommendations.

(3) Since London has machinery for consulting Dominion Governments and since Dutch Government is in London the British Government will be responsible for obtaining their views and agreement and for including these in the final telegrams to Washington.

(4) Agreement having been reached between President and Prime Minister and Minister of Defence the orders to Supreme Commander will be despatched from Washington in the name of both of them.

APPENDIX SIX

Dutch Warships in the Netherlands East Indies on January 10th, 1942

Light cruisers: 4
Destroyers: 7
Submarines: 11
Gunboats: 2
Minelayers: 8
Minesweepers: 8
Auxiliary minesweepers: 22
Motor torpedo boats: 10 (Two were added on February 17th.)
Militarised auxiliary ships: 19 (These were used for patrol, escort, inspection and similar duties.)
Surveying ships: 3
Supply ships and submarine depot ships: 2
Patrol boats: 23
Anti-submarine vessels (Four anti-submarine vessels were commissioned on February 1st.)
Guard vessels: 8 (Two were added on January 17th and one at the end of February.)
Examination vessels: 13
Torpedo workship: 1
Anti-aircraft vessels: 9
MTB depot ships: 2
Hospital ship: 1
Tugs: about 25
Barracks ship: 1
Tankers: 14

APPENDIX SEVEN

Dutch Naval Aircraft in the Netherlands East Indies on January 10th, 1942

The Royal Netherlands Naval Air Service had no fighters, only bombers, reconnaissance aircraft, which could also be used as bombers, and trainers. The cruisers *De Ruyter* and *Java* could each take two sea reconnaissance planes on board; *De Ruyter* had one catapult. During actions, however, it was impossible to keep the aircraft on board. The destroyers could each carry one seaplane, but as this meant that X and Y guns could not be used, they were never taken aboard.

Name	*Type*	*Identification-letter*	*Number*	*Arrival of the first aircraft in the Netherlands Indies*	*Particulars*
(1) Fokker T-IV-W	Twin-engined bomber	T	10	1926	Designed to carry one torpedo but never used as such.
(2) Dornier 24 K	Three-engined reconnaissance aircraft	X	28	1937	
(3) Catalina	Twin-engined reconnaissance aircraft	Y	30	1941	
(4) Dornier Wal	Twin-engined reconnaissance aircraft	D	11	1926	
(5) Fokker C-VII-W	Single-engined reconnaissance aircraft	V	6	1938	
(6) Fokker C-XI-W	Single-engined reconnaissance aircraft	W	7	1936	Could be carried aboard the cruisers.
(7) STM-32 Ryan	Single-engined trainer	S	40	1940	
(8) Tiger Moth	Single-engined trainer	—	5	?	
(9) Fokker C-XIV-W	Single-engined trainer	F	11	1940	

APPENDIX EIGHT

Losses of Main Dutch Warships between January 10th and March 8th, 1942

Name	*Type*	*Date of loss*	*Place of loss*	*Number of men killed*
Java	Cruiser	February 27th	06°00'South 112°05'East	509
De Ruyter	Cruiser	February 27th	06°00'South 112°05'East	345
Van Ghent	Destroyer	February 15th	03°05'South 107°21.5'East	—
Evertsen	Destroyer	March 1st	05°55'South 105°30'East	32
Piet Hein	Destroyer	February 19th	08°40'South 115°20'East	64
Kortenaer	Destroyer	February 27th	06°29'South 112°05'East	56
Witte de With	Destroyer	March 2nd	Naval Base Surabaya (scuttled)	1
Banckert	Destroyer	March 2nd	Naval Base Surabaya (scuttled)	—
Van Nes	Destroyer	February 17th	03°27'South 106°38'East	68
K VII	Submarine	February 18th	Naval Base Surabaya	13
K X	Submarine	March 2nd	Naval Base Surabaya (scuttled)	—
K XIII	Submarine	March 2nd	Naval Base Surabaya (scuttled)	—
K XVIII	Submarine	March 2nd	Naval Base Surabaya (scuttled)	—
Soerabaja	Gunboat	February 18th	Naval Base Surabaya	7
Pro Patria	Minelayer	February 15th	Musi River	1
Krakatau	Minelayer	March 8th	Naval Base Surabaya	—
Prins van Oranje	Minelayer	January 11th	North of Tarakan	102
Gouden Leeuw	Minelayer	March 7th	Naval Base Surabaya (scuttled)	—
Soemenep	Minelayer	March 2nd	Naval Base Surabaya (scuttled)	—

Name	*Type*	*Date of loss*	*Place of loss*	*Number of men killed*
Bangkalan	Minelayer	March 2nd	Naval Base Surabaya (scuttled)	—
Rigel	Minelayer	March 2nd	Naval Base Surabaya (scuttled)	—
A	Minesweeper	March 1st	Naval Base Surabaya	—
B	Minesweeper	March 1st	Naval Base Surabaya	—
C	Minesweeper	March 6th	Naval Base Surabaya (scuttled)	—
D	Minesweeper	March 6th	Naval Base Surabaya (scuttled)	—
Pieter de Bitter	Minesweeper	March 6th	Naval Base Surabaya (scuttled)	—
Eland Dubois	Minesweeper	March 8th	Madura Strait (scuttled)	—
Jan van Amstel	Minesweeper	March 8th	40 miles north of Bali	23
Endeh	Auxiliary minesweeper	March 2nd	65 miles south of Billiton	9

On March 2nd and 3rd eighteen auxiliary minesweepers were scuttled at Tandjong Priok and Surabaya.

APPENDIX NINE

Losses of the Main Naval Aircraft of the Royal Netherlands Navy in the Netherlands East Indies (January 10th – March 8th, 1942)

Name	*Date of loss*	*Place of loss*
X-1	March 3rd	Broome (in Australia) by Japanese action.
X-3	March 3rd	Broome by Japanese action.
X-6	February 3rd	Morokrembangan (base of the Royal Netherlands Naval Air) by Japanese action.
X-13	February 7th	Near Roti by Japanese action.
X-14	January 23rd	Balikpapan; crashed.
X-16	March 1st	Tandjong Priok. After Japanese bombardment destroyed by own naval personnel.
X-17	February 24th	Shot down during air battle near Noordwachter.
X-18	February 24th	Shot down during air battle near Noordwachter.
X-19	January 25th	Near Menari; crashed.
X-20	March 3rd	Broome by Japanese action.
X-21	February 23rd	Above Oostervaarwater (Surabaya) by Japanese action.
X-22	February 5th	Morokrembangan by Japanese action.
X-23	March 3rd	Broome by Japanese action.
X-28	March 3rd	Broome by Japanese action.
X-29	February 11th	South of Bawean; emergency landing.
X-30	February 3rd	Morokrembangan by Japanese action.
X-31	February 5th	Morokrembangan by Japanese action.
X-32	February 7th	Near Roti by Japanese action.
X-33	February 5th	Morokrembangan by Japanese action.
X-35	February 7th	Near Roti by Japanese action.
X-36	March 5th	South of Broome. Destroyed by own naval personnel.

Name	*Date of loss*	*Place of loss*
X-37	February 3rd	Morokrembangan after Japanese bombardment destroyed by own naval personnel.

Six Dornier aircraft managed to escape to Australia.

Name	*Date of loss*	*Place of loss*
Y-38	February 9th	Westervaarwater (Surabaya). After an emergency landing.
Y-39	February 5th	Morokrembangan by Japanese action.
Y-40	February 3rd	Shot down while flying over Strait Madura.
Y-41	March 3rd	Morokrembangan. Destroyed by own naval personnel.
Y-42	March 1st	Morokrembangan. Heavily damaged by Japanese action and destroyed by own naval personnel.
Y-43	February 5th	Morokrembangan by Japanese action.
Y-46	March 1st	Morokrembangan by Japanese action.
Y-47	February 23rd	At Tandjong Priok after an emergency landing at night.
Y-48	March 3rd	Destroyed by own naval personnel at Tandjong Priok after a Japanese bombardment.
Y-50	February 5th	Morokrembangan by Japanese action.
Y-51	January 21st	On the Barito River (Borneo) by Japanese action.
Y-58	January 11th	Shot down during air battle near Kema.
Y-59	March 3rd	Broome by Japanese action.
Y-60	March 3rd	Broome by Japanese action.
Y-61	February 3rd	Morokrembangan by Japanese action.
Y-63	February 27th	Shot down during air battle near Noord Gebroeders.
Y-65	February 27th	Heavily damaged after air battle south of Tjilatjap and written off.
Y-66	March 4th	Tjilatjap by Japanese action.
Y-67	March 3rd	Broome by Japanese action.
Y-70	March 3rd	Broome by Japanese action.
Y-72	February 5th	Shot down between Waru and Sidoardjo by Japanese aircraft.
Y-73	March 3rd	Morokrembangan destroyed by own naval personnel.

Three Dutch Catalina aircraft, and a damaged American Catalina, which was left behind and given the number *Y-3*, escaped to Australia, four to Colombo.

All other aircraft were either destroyed by the bombardments on Surabaya or by own naval personnel at the beginning of March. On February 17th, 1942 33 Ryan aircraft were shipped from Java to Australia by the motor vessel *Tjinegara*.

APPENDIX TEN

Japanese Ships Sunk in the Netherlands East Indies by the Allies (January 10th – March 8th, 1942)

Date	*Name (tonnage)*	*Type*	*Positions*	*By*	*Type*
January 10th	*Akita Maru* (3,817brt)	Passenger-Cargo	07°35' North 120°50' East	*Sculpin*	Submarine
January 12th	*W 13* (492)	Minesweeper	Off Tarakan	Dutch coastal battery at Tarakan	
January 12th	*W 14* (492)	Minesweeper	Off Tarakan	Dutch coastal battery at Tarakan	
January 17th	*I 60* (1,635)	Submarine	06°00' South 105°00' East	*Jupiter*	Destroyer
January 23rd	*Nana Maru* (6,764brt)	Passenger-Cargo	00°10' North 118°00' East	Aircraft	Dutch bomber
January 23rd	*Tsuruga Maru* (6,988brt)	Passenger-Cargo	Off Balikpapan	*K XVIII*	Submarine
January 24th	*Sumanoura Maru* (3,519brt)	Passenger-Cargo	Off Balikpapan	*John D. Ford*,	
January 24th	*Tatsukami Maru* (7,064brt)	Passenger-Cargo	Off Balikpapan	*Pope*, *Parrott*,	Destroyers
January 24th	*Kuretake Maru* (5,175brt)	Passenger-Cargo	Off Balikpapan	*Paul Jones*	
January 24th	*Myoken Maru* (4,124brt)	Cargo	01°22' North 125°05' East	Swordfish	Submarine
February 2nd	*W 9* (630)	Minesweeper	Off Ambon	Dutch mines	—
February 9th.	*Natsushio* (2,000)	Destroyer	05°36' South 119°06' East	*S 37*	Submarine
February 14th	*Inabasan Maru* (989brt)	Cargo	01°25' South 105°00' East	Aircraft	Unknown
March 1st	*W 2* (630)	Minesweeper	Bantam Bay	Unknown*	—
March 1st	*Sakura Maru* (7,170brt)	Cargo	Bantam Bay	Unknown*	—

*According to Japanese sources both the *W 2* and the *Sakura Maru* were sunk by torpedoes from friendly ships, probably the *Fubuki*.

APPENDIX ELEVEN

Allied Ships which were in the Waters of the Netherlands East Indies (January 10th – March 8th, 1942)

Name	*Type*	*Year of launching*	*Main armament*	*Particulars*
British				
Exeter	Heavy cruiser	1929	6 x 20.3cm (8in) 6 x 53.3cm (21in) (torpedo tubes)	Lost March 1st
Dragon	Light cruiser	1917	6 x 15.2cm (6in)	
Danae	Light cruiser	1918	12 x 53.3cm (21in) (torpedo tubes)	
Tenedos	Destroyer	1918	3 x 10.2cm (4in)	
Scout	Destroyer	1918	4 x 53.3cm (21in) (torpedo tubes)	
Stronghold	Destroyer	1919		Lost March 2nd
Electra	Destroyer	1933	4 x 12cm (4.7in)	Lost February 27th
Encounter	Destroyer	1937	8 x 53.3cm (21in) (torpedo tubes)	Lost March 1st
Jupiter	Destroyer	1938	6 x 12cm (4.7in) 10 x 53.3cm (21in) (torpedo tubes)	Lost February 27th
Truant	Submarine	1939	10 x 53.3cm (21in) (torpedo tubes)	
Trusty	Submarine	1941	11 x 53.3cm (21in) (torpedo tubes)	
War Sirdar	Oiler	1920	—	Lost February 28th
Wo Kwang	Auxiliary minesweeper	1927	—	
Rahman	Auxiliary minesweeper	1926	—	Lost March 1st
Gemas	Auxiliary minesweeper	1925	—	Sunk March 2nd by own crew
Francol	Oiler	1917	—	Lost March 4th
Wollongong	Sloop	1941	1 x 10.2cm (4in)	
Anking	Base and accom-modation ship	1925	—	Lost March 4th
Scott Harley	Auxiliary minesweeper	1913	—	Lost March 3rd
Seram				
MMS 51				Lost March 4th
Australian				
Perth	Light cruiser	1934	8 x 15.2cm (6in)	Lost March 1st
Hobart	Light cruiser	1934	8 x 53.3cm (21in) (torpedo tubes)	
Yarra	Escort sloop	1935	3 x 10.2cm (4in) AA	Lost March 4th
Bendigo	Fleet minesweeper	1941	1 x 10.2cm (4in)	
Ballarat	Fleet minesweeper	1940		
Burnie	Fleet minesweeper	1940		
Maryborough	Fleet minesweeper	1940		
Toowoomba	Fleet minesweeper	1941		
Gouldburn	Fleet minesweeper	1940		
Indian				
Jumna	Escort sloop	1940	6 x 10.2cm (4in) AA	
American				
Houston	Heavy cruiser	1929	9 x 20.3cm (8in)	Lost March 1st
Marblehead	Light cruiser	1923	10 x 15.2cm (6in) 6 x 53.3cm (21in) (torpedo tubes)	

Name	*Type*	*Year of launching*	*Main armament*	*Particulars*
Boise	Light cruiser	1936	15 x 15.2cm (6in)	
Langley	Seaplane tender	1912	4 x 12.7cm (5in) 16 aircraft	Lost February 27th
Barker	Destroyers	1919	4 x 10.2cm (4in)	
Bulmer		1920	12 x 53.3cm (21in) (torpedo tubes)	
Edsall		1920		Lost March 1st
John D. Edwards		1919		
John D. Ford		1920		
Parrott		1919		
Paul Jones		1920		
Peary		1920		Lost February 19th
Pillsbury		1920		Lost March 1st
Pope		1920		Lost March 1st
Stewart		1920		Lost March 2nd
Whipple		1919		
Alden		1919		
Shark	Submarine	1935	6 x 53.3cm (21in) (torpedo tubes)	Lost in February, probably on the 11th off Menado
Salmon	Submarines	1937	8 x 53.3cm (21in) (torpedo tubes)	
Seal		1937		
Skipjack		1937		
Snapper		1937		
Stingray		1937		
Sturgeon		1938		
Sargo		1938		
Saury		1938		
Spearfish		1938		
Sculpin		1938		
Sailfish	Submarines	1938	8 x 53.3cm (21in) (torpedo tubes)	
Swordfish		1939		
Seadragon		1939		
Searaven		1939		
Seawolf		1939		
S 36	Submarines	1922	4 x 53.3cm (21in) (torpedo tubes)	Lost January 20th
S 37		1922		
S 38		1922		
S 39		1922		
S 40		1922		
S 41		1923		
Porpoise	Submarines	1935	6 x 53.3cm (21in) (torpedo tubes)	
Pike		1935		
Pickerel		1936		
Perch		1936		Lost March 3rd
Permit		1936		
Tarpon	Submarine	1935	6 x 53.3cm (21in) (torpedo tubes)	
Childs	Seaplane tender	1920	2 x 10.2cm (4in)	
William B. Preston	Seaplane tender	1919	2 x 10.2cm (4in)	
Holland	Submarine tender	1926	8 x 12.7cm (5in) 1 x 53.3cm (21in) (torpedo tubes)	
Canopus	Submarine tender	1919	2 x 12.7cm (5in)	
Pecos	Oiler	1921	4 x 12.7cm (5in)	Lost March 1st
Gold Star	Oiler	1920	2 x 12.7cm (5in)	
Black Hawk	Destroyer tender	1913	4 x 12.7cm (5in)	
Heron	Seaplane tender	1918	2 x 7.6cm (3in)	
Whippoorwill	Minesweeper	1919	2 x 7.6cm (3in) AA	
Lark	Minesweeper	1918	2 x 7.6cm (3in) AA	
Isabel	Patrol vessel	1917	2 x 7.6cm (3in)	
Asheville	Gunboats	1918	3 x 10.2cm (4in)	Lost March 3rd
Tulsa		1922		
Trinity	Oiler	1920	2 x 12.7cm (5in)	
Lanakai	Patrol vessel			
Wakefield	Transport	1932	4 x 12.7cm (5in)	
Otus	Submarine tender	1940	4 x 12.7cm (5in)	

APPENDIX TWELVE

Comparison of Allied and Japanese Ships, which Took Part in the Battle of the Java Sea

Combined Striking Force

Type	*Name*	*Year of building (launching)*	*Armament*	*Armour*	*Speed*	*Tonnage*
Heavy cruiser	*Houston*	1929	9 x 20.3cm (8in) * 8 x 12.7cm (5in) 2 x 4.7cm (3pdrs) 8 x 40mm AA	Vertical side 76mm (3in)	32.7 knots	9,050 tons
Heavy cruiser	*Exeter*	1929	6 x 20.3cm (8in) 8 x 10.2cm (4in) AA 10 x 4cm (2pdrs) AA 6 torpedo tubes 53.3cm (21in)	Side 76.51mm (3in) Deck 51mm (2in)	32.2 knots	8,390 tons

* Due to a bomb hit on February 4th the after turret (3 x 20.3cm, 8in) was still out of action, so that *Houston* really had only 6 x 20.3cm (8in).

Type	*Name*	*Year of building (launching)*	*Armament*	*Armour*	*Speed*	*Tonnage*
Light cruiser	*De Ruyter*	1935	7 x 15cm (5.9in) 10 x 40mm AA	Side 50.60mm (2-3in) Deck 35mm (1¼in)	32.0 knots	6,470 tons
Light cruiser	*Java*	1921	10 x 15cm (5.9in) 8 x 40mm AA	Side 75mm (2-3in) Deck 50.25mm (1-2in)	31.3 knots	6,670 tons
Light cruiser	*Perth*	1934	8 x 15.2cm (6in) 8 x 10.2cm (4in) AA 4 x 4.7cm (3pdrs) 8 torpedo tubes 53.3cm (21in)	Side 76.51mm (2-3in) Deck 51mm (2in)	32.5 knots	7,040 tons
Destroyer	*Jupiter*	1938	6 x 12cm (4.7in) * 1 x 10.2cm (4in) 4 x 40mm AA 10 torpedo tubes 53.3cm (21in)	—	36.0 knots	1,690 tons
Destroyers	*Electra* *Encounter*	1934 1934	4 x 12cm (4.7in) 1 x 10.2cm (4in) 8 torpedo tubes 53.3cm (21in)	—	35.5 knots	1,375 tons
Destroyer	*Witte de With*	1930	4 x 12cm (4.7in) 1 x 7.5cm (3in) 4 x 40mm AA 6 torpedo tubes 53.3cm (21in)	—	34 knots	1,315 tons

* In the action in Sunda Strait on January 17th one of the twin guns of 12cm (4.7in) had been taken off for repairs and replaced by a single gun, so that *Jupiter* had 5 x 12cm (4.7in).

Type	*Name*	*Year of building (launching)*	*Armament*	*Armour*	*Speed*	*Tonnage*
Destroyer	*Kortenaer*	1926	4 x 12cm (4.7in) 2 x 7.5cm (3in) 6 torpedo tubes 53.3cm (21in)	—	34 knots*	1,326 tons
Destroyers	*Alden* *John D. Edwards* *John D. Ford* *Paul Jones*	1919 1919 1920 1920	4 x 10.2cm (4in) 1 x 7.6cm (3in) 12 torpedo tubes 53.3cm (21in)	—	35 knots	1,190 tons

*Due to a boiler defect the maximum speed of *Kortanaer* was only 27 knots.

Japanese Force*

Type	*Name*	*Year of building (launching)*	*Armament*	*Armour*	*Speed*	*Tonnage*
Heavy cruisers	*Nachi* *Haguro*	1927 1928	10 x 20.3cm (8in) 8 x 12cm (5in) AA 8 x 25mm AA 16 torpedo tubes 60.9cm (24in)	Side 76mm (3in) Deck 76.51mm (2-3in)	33 knots	13,000 tons

*As a primary source *The Japanese Imperial Navy* by Dr E. Lacroix has been used. See also *Japanese Battleships and Cruisers* and *Japanese Aircraft Carriers and Destroyers* both published by MacDonald, London in 1964.

Type	*Name*	*Year of building (launching)*	*Armament*	*Armour*	*Speed*	*Tonnage*
Light cruisers	*Jintsu* *Naka*	1923 1925	7 x 14cm (5.5in) 2 x 12cm (5in) 8 torpedo tubes 60.9cm (24in)	Side 51mm (2in) Deck 51-63mm (2½in)	33 knots	5,850 tons
Destroyers	*Yukikaze* *Amatsukaze* *Tokitsukaze* *Hatsukaze*	1939 1939 1939 1939	6 x 12.7cm (5in) 4 x 25mm AA 8 torpedo tubes 60.9cm (24in)	—	35 knots	2,033 tons
Destroyers	*Asagumo* *Minegumo*	1937 1937	6 x 12.7cm (5in) 4 x 25mm AA 8 torpedo tubes 60.9cm (24in)	—	35 knots	1,961 tons
Destroyers	*Yamakaze* *Kawakaze* *Yudachi* *Harusame* *Samidare* *Murasame*	1936 1936 1936 1935 1935 1935	5 x 12.7cm (5in) 4 x 25mm AA 8 torpedo tubes 60.9cm (24in)	—	34 knots	1,685 tons
Destroyers	*Sazanami* *Ushio*	1931 1930	6 x 12.7cm (5in) 4 x 25mm AA 9 torpedo tubes 60.9cm (24in)	—	38 knots	1,750 tons

Comparisons Between the Forces

Comparative Armament of both Forces

	Allied	*Japanese*
Guns:		
8in	12	20
6in (approximately)	25	14
5in (approximately)	29	98
4in (approximately)	35	—
Torpedo tubes:		
24in	—	162
21in	100	—

The Japanese were thus in all respects superior to the allies as opposed to the view of the experts in 1942.

	Allied	*Japanese*
Tonnage (approximately)	50,000	65,000
Oil	Half or less	More than ¾ full
Ammunition	Probably ¾	Full

Other Comparisons Between the two Forces

DEGREE OF TRAINING

Allied: Sufficient. The crews of each individual ship were well trained, but the ships themselves had not had sufficient training as a team. The *Perth* for instance only arrived in the Netherlands East Indies on February 24th, 1942.

Japanese: Very good. The Japanese had a fleet, which was well trained and extremely well co-ordinated.

MORALE

Allied: Good. The crews of the allied ships were utterly exhausted by their utmost exertion of the previous days. The native personnel aboard the Dutch ships had behaved very well. For some days the crews had to do without a hot meal, as cooks and stewards were detailed at the guns, the bringing up of ammunition, etc. Because the ships had sailed for some days at action stations, it had not been possible to provide a meal of any substance. The fact that morale was good was proved when the ships sailed on February 27th, 1942. Not one member—European or native—had missed his ship, even though everybody knew exactly what was going to happen.

Japanese: Very good. The crews were well rested. Up to the moment of the encounter the Japanese had experienced little resistance.

STATE OF THE SHIPS

Allied: Sufficient to good. The *Kortenaer* could only make a maximum speed of 27 knots because of boiler defects and this determined the speed of the entire Combined Striking Force.

Japanese: Good to very good.

NUMBER OF MEN	*Allied*	*Japanese*
(approx.)	4,100	5,250

FURTHER PARTICULARS

Allied: The *Exeter* was equipped with a radio direction finder. The allied ships had no radar. There was no reconnaissance from the air.

Japanese: The Japanese had no radar, but they received valuable information from reconnaissance aircraft.

APPENDIX FOURTEEN

Torpedoes Launched by Japanese Ships During the Battle of the Java Sea on February 27th, 1942

Name ship	*Times of launching*			*Number of torpedoes launched*		
Naka	4	4	—	16.33	17.50	—
Jintsu	4	4	4	16.35	17.54	19.36
Asagumo	3	4	—	16.40	18.07	—
Minegumo	8	—	—	16.42	—	—
Murasame	4	4	—	16.45	18.04	—
Samidare	4	4	—	16.45	18.04	—
Harusame	4	4	—	16.45	18.04	—
Yudachi	4	4	—	16.45	18.04	—
Haguro	8	8	4	16.52	17.48	23.23
Nachi	—	8	8	—	17.54	23.22
Yukikaze	—	8	—	—	17.57	—
Amatsukaze	—	8	—	—	17.57	—
Tokitsukaze	—	8	—	—	17.58	—
Hatsukaze	—	8	—	—	17.58	—
Yamakaze	—	8	—	—	18.00	—
Kawikaze	—	8	—	—	18.02	—
Total				43	92	16

All ships had spare torpedoes aboard so that the tubes could be reloaded after the first attack.

Minegumo was the only ship that did not launch her torpedoes as she had to carry out evasive action to avoid torpedoes launched by the other Japanese ships.

It is interesting to note that the *Nachi* did not launch her torpedoes, because the stop-valve for the compressed air system had accidentally been opened too long before the moment of launching. When the order for firing the torpedoes was given there was no air left.

APPENDIX FIFTEEN

Torpedoes Launched by Japanese Ships During the Battle of Bantam Bay on February 28th, 1942

Name of ship	*Times of launching*		*Number of torpedoes launched*	
Fubuki	23.15	—	9	—
Hatsuyuki	23.40	—	9	—
Shirayuki	23.40	—	9	—
Asakaze	23.43	—	6	—
Natori	23.44	—	4	—
Mikuma	23.49	—	6	—
Mogami	23.49	23.57	6	6
Harukaze	—	23.56	—	5
Hatakaze	—	23.57	—	6
Shirakumo	—	24.00	—	9
Murakumo	—	24.00	—	9
Shikinami	—	00.29	—	1
Total			49	36

APPENDIX SIXTEEN

Torpedoes Launched by Japanese Ships During the Encounter with the Exeter *on March 1st, 1942*

Name of ship	*Times of launching*		*Number of torpedoes launched*	
Kawakaze	11.19	—	2	—
Haguro	11.20	—	4	—
Yamakaze	11.21	—	4	—
Nachi	11.22	—	4	—
Ashigara	11.30	—	?	—
Inazuma	?	?	2	2
Total			16(?)	2

APPENDIX SEVENTEEN

Losses of Personnel During the Battle of the Java Sea and the Battle of Bantam Bay

Battle of the Java Sea

Name of the ship	*Killed*	*Wounded*	*Saved*	*Total crew*
De Ruyter	about 345	—	about 92	437
Java	about 509	—	about 19	528
Kortenaer	56	—	94	150
Exeter	14	—	—	650
Jupiter	—	—	183	183
Electra	91	—	54	145
Total allies	about 1,015	—	about 442	2,093
Jintsu	1	about 4	—	450
Asagumo	5	19	—	250
Minegumo	—	4	—	250
Ushio	a few	a few	—	200
Sasanami	a few	a few	—	200
Total Japanese	about 10	about 30	—	1,350

Battle of Bantam Bay

Name of the ship	*Killed*	*Wounded*	*Saved*	*Total crew*
Houston	696	—	368	1,064
Perth	375	—	307	682
Total allies	1,071	—	675	1,746
W 2	35	9	—	—
Mikuma	6	11	—	—
Shirayuki	1	8	—	—
Harukaze	3	5	—	—
Total Japanese	45	33	—	—

Bibliography

R. de Belot; *La guerre aéronavale du Pacifique (1941-1945);* Payot, Paris, 1957

K. W. L. Bezemer; *Zij vochten op de zeven zeeën;* Uitgeversmaatschappij W. de Haan N.V., Utrecht, 1954

J. W. T. Bosch; *De militaire luchtvaart van het Koninklijk Nederlands Indisch leger in oorlog, 8 december 1941-9 maart 1942;* Manuscript, Ypenburg, 1973

L. H. Brereton; *The Brereton Diaries;* William Morrow and Company, New York, 1946

Bureau maritieme historie; *De Japanese opmars naar en in Nederlands-Indië en de acties op de maritieme steunpunten in de buitengewesten;* Manuscript, 's-Gravenhage, 1961

Bureau maritieme historie; *Ingedeelde chronologie, Oost-Indië, 10 december 1941-8 maart 1942;* Manuscript, 's-Gravenhage, 1963

Bureau maritieme historie; *Operaties der Nederlandse onderzeeboten onder bevel CZM in de Indische wateren benevens de bewegingen der Engelse en Amerikaanse onderzeeboten in het tijdvak december 1941-maart 1942;* Manuscript, 's-Gravenhage, 1958

Bureau maritieme historie; *Verrichtingen van de MLD in Nederlands Oost-Indië gedurende de Japanse opmars;* Manuscript, 's-Gravenhage, 1962

T. J. Cain; *H.M.S. Electra;* Frederick Muller Ltd, London, 1959

W. R. Carter; *Beans, Bullets, and Black Oil;* US Government Printing Office, Washington, 1951

W. S. Churchill; *The Second World War. Volume IV: The Hinge of Fate;* Cassell and Co Ltd, London, 1951

J. F. van Dulm en L. L. von Münching; *"De materieelverliezen der Koninlijke marine in de tweede wereldoorlog, 1939-1945"; Marineblad,* Volume 78, 1968, pages 351-412

G. H. Gill; *Royal Australian Navy, 1939-1942;* Australian War Memorial, Canberra, 1957

D. Gillison; *Royal Australian Air Force, 1939-1942;* Australian War Memorial, Canberra, 1962

O. L. Gordon; *Fight it out;* William Kimber, London, 1957

J. M. Gwyer and J. R. M. Butler; *Grand Strategy. Volume III. June 1941-August 1942;* Her Majesty's Stationery Office, London, 1964

C. E. L. Helfrich; *Memoires. Eerste deel: De Maleise Barrière;* Elsevier, Amsterdam, 1950

H. Ito and R. Pineau; *The End of the Imperial Japanese Navy;* Norton, New York, 1962

W. Karig and W. Kelley; *Battle Report. Pearl Harbour to Coral Sea;* Rhinehart and Company, Inc, New York, 1944

E. J. King and W. M. Whitehill; *Fleet Admiral King, a naval record;* Norton, New York, 1952

A. Kroese; *Neerland's Zeemacht in Oorlog;* The Netherlands Publishing Company, London, 1944

E. Lacroix; "The Japanese Imperial Navy"; *The Belgian Shiplover,* Numbers 71, 73, 76, 81, 85, 87, 90, 96 and 97

F. M. McGuire; *The Royal Australian Navy;* Oxford University Press, Melbourne, 1948

S. E. Morison; *History of United States Naval Operations in World War II. Volume III. The Rising Sun in the Pacific, 1931-April 1942;* Little, Brown and Company, Boston, 1948

F. C. van Oosten; "De slag in de Javazee, 27 februari-1 maart 1942" *Marineblad,* Volume 77, 1967, pages 151-213

J. P. H. Perks; Kruisers en vliegtuigen" *Marineblad,* Volume 51, 1936, pages 736-771

John Deane Potter; *Admiral of the Pacific. The Life of Yamamoto;* William Heinemann Ltd, London, 1965

W. D. Puleston; *The Influence of Sea Power in World War II;* Yale University Press, New Haven, London, 1947

H. V. Quispel; *Nederlandsch-Indië in den Tweeden Wereldoorlog;* London, 1945

Theodore Roscoe; *United States Destroyer Operations in World War II;* US Naval Institute, Annapolis, 1953

Theodore Roscoe; *United States Submarine Operations in World War II;* US Naval Institute, Annapolis, 1950

S. W. Roskill; *The War at Sea, 1939-1945. Volume II. The Period of Balance;* Her Majesty's Stationery Office, London, 1956

Friedrich Ruge; *Entscheidung im Pazifik;* Rütten & Loening Verlag, Hamburg, 1951

G. W. Stöve; "Queen's Navy at War"; *US Naval Institute Proceedings,* Volume 76, 1950, pages 288-301

F. van der Straaten; "Enige bespiegelingen over de slag in de Javazee (27 februari 1942)"; *Marineblad,* Volume 77, 1967, pages 325-341

Lord Strabolgi; *Singapore and After;* Hutchinson and Co, London, 1942

A. G. Vromans; *Gegevens betreffende de Japanse Keizerlijke marine in de Indische wateren gedurende de tweede wereldoorlog;* Manuscript, Amsterdam, 1963

A. G. Vromans; *Gevecht in de Java-Zee op 27/28 februari 1942;* Stenciled, Amsterdam, 1961-1965

S. Woodburn Kirby; *The War against Japan, Volume I. The Loss of Singapore;* Her Majesty's Stationery Office, London, 1957

Index